LINQ Quickly

A practical guide to programming Language Integrated Query with C#

N Satheesh Kumar

PUBLISHING

BIRMINGHAM - MUMBAI

LINQ Quickly

First published: November 2007

Production Reference: 1161107

Published by Packt Publishing Ltd.
32 Lincoln Road
Olton
Birmingham, B27 6PA, UK.

ISBN 978-1-847192-54-7

www.packtpub.com

Cover Image by Vinayak Chittar (vinayak.chittar@gmail.com)

Credits

Author

N Satheesh Kumar

Reviewer

Granville Barnett

Senior Acquisition Editor

Douglas Paterson

Development Editor

Nikhil Bangera

Technical Editor

Sarvesh Shanbhag

Editorial Manager

Dipali Chittar

Project Manager

Abhijeet Deobhakta

Project Coordinator

Patricia Weir

Indexer

Hemangini Bari

Proofreader

Cathy Cumberlidge

Production Coordinators

Aparna Bhagat

Shantanu Zagade

Cover Designer

Aparna Bhagat

About the Author

N Satheesh Kumar has a Bachelor's Degree in Computer Science Engineering and has around eleven years of experience in software development lifecycle, project and program management. He started his career developing software applications using Borland software products in a company based in India, and then moved to the United Arab Emirates where he continued developing custom application software using Borland Delphi, and customizing Great Plain Dynamics (now known as Microsoft Dynamics) for an automobile company. He moved back to India and spent three years in design and developing application software using Microsoft products for a top multi national company, and then spent a couple of years in project management and program management activities. Now he works as a Technical Architect for a top retail company based in the United States. He works with the latest Microsoft technologies and has published many articles on LINQ and other features of .NET.

About the Reviewer

Granville Barnett's interest in programming has spanned many languages; his talents have been applied most notably at Microsoft. Granville has worked with LINQ since the LINQ May 2006 CTP and has since then advised some of the biggest companies in the world on the successful application of LINQ. Granville has a very active interest in data structures and algorithms, and compiler theory, design and implementation.

He would like to thank all at Microsoft, in particular the members of the UK Application Development Consulting team.

As an author, Granville has written several magazine and web articles on LINQ.

He can be reached through his website at `http://gbarnett.org`.

Table of Contents

Preface

Language Integrated Query (LINQ) is a new feature in Visual Studio 2008 that extends its query capabilities using C# and Visual Basic. Visual Studio 2008 comes with LINQ provider assemblies that enable the use of LINQ with data sources, such as in-memory collections, SQL relational databases, ADO.NET Datasets, XML documents, etc. In Visual Studio 2008, Visual C# and Visual Basic are the languages that implement the LINQ language extensions. LINQ language extensions use the new standard query operators, API, which is the query language for any collection that implements `IEnumerable<T>`.

This book introduces the reader to the basic concepts of LINQ, and takes them through using LINQ with an example-driven approach.

What This Book Covers

Chapter 1 looks at the overall features of LINQ, and gives an overview of different operators provided by LINQ to operate on objects, XML, relational databases, etc.

Chapter 2 examines LINQ to Objects, which means that you can use LINQ to query objects in a collection. Using this feature, you can access in-memory data structures using LINQ. You can directly query collections, and filter out required values without using powerful filtering, ordering, and grouping capabilities.

Chapter 3 looks at LINQ to XML. It is a new in-memory XML programming API to work against XML data. There are different ways of creating XML trees in .NET. LINQ to XML is the new method of creating and manipulating XML data through .NET. The properties and methods of LINQ help in navigating and manipulating XML elements and attributes.

Chapter 4, which covers LINQ to SQL, takes care of translating LINQ expressions into equivalent T-SQL, passing it onto the database for execution, and then returning the results back to the calling application. It reduces programming time and comes with two different design-time tools, which are used for converting relational database objects into object definitions. It also has the ability to create databases, and database objects.

Chapter 5 examines LINQ to DataSets. An ADO.NET DataSet provides a disconnected data source environment for applications. It can be used with multiple data sources. A DataSet has the flexibility of handling data locally in cache memory where the application resides. The application can continue working with a DataSet when it is disconnected from the source and is not dependent on the availability of the data source. The DataSet maintains information about the changes made to data so that updates can be tracked and sent back to the database as soon as the data source is available or reconnected.

Chapter 6 covers LINQ to XSD. It enhances XML programming by adding the feature of typed views on un-typed XML trees. LINQ to XSD gives a better programming environment by providing the object models generated from XML schemas. This is called typed XML programming.

Chapter 7 looks at standard query operators provided by LINQ, and how you can use some of them against different data sources.

Appendix A takes you through building a simple ASP.NET application using LINQ.

Appendix B tells you how to access Outlook objects using LINQ.

Conventions

In this book, you will find a number of styles of text that distinguish between different kinds of information. Here are some examples of these styles, and an explanation of their meaning.

There are three styles for code. Code words in text are shown as follows: "LINQ queries work on sources which are IEnumerable<>. The new ADO.NET provides a feature for getting the rows enumerated by applying AsEnumerable() on DataTables."

A block of code will be set as follows:

```
public class Icecream
{
  public string Name { get; set; }
  public double Price { get; set; }
}
```

New terms and **important words** are introduced in a bold-type font.

Words that you see on the screen, in menus or dialog boxes, for example, appear in our text like this: "You can see DataTables listed in the **DataSet Visualizer**."

Reader Feedback

Feedback from our readers is always welcome. Let us know what you think about this book, what you liked or disliked. Reader feedback is important for us to develop titles that you get the most out of.

To send us general feedback, simply drop an email to feedback@packtpub.com, making sure to mention the book title in the subject of your message.

If there is a book that you need and would like to see us publish, please send us a note in the **SUGGEST A TITLE** form on www.packtpub.com or email www.packtpub.com/authors.

If there is a topic that you have expertise in and you are interested in either writing or contributing to a book, see our author guide on www.packtpub.com/authors.

Customer Support

Now that you are the proud owner of a Packt book, we have a number of things to help you to get the most from your purchase.

Downloading the Example Code for the Book

Visit http://www.packtpub.com/support, and select this book from the list of titles to download any example code or extra resources for this book. The files available for download will then be displayed.

The downloadable files contain instructions on how to use them.

Errata

Although we have taken every care to ensure the accuracy of our contents, mistakes do happen. If you find a mistake in one of our books — maybe a mistake in text or code — we would be grateful if you would report this to us. By doing this you can save other readers from frustration, and help to improve subsequent versions of this book. If you find any errata, report them by visiting http://www.packtpub.com/support, selecting your book, clicking on the **Submit Errata** link, and entering the details of your errata. Once your errata are verified, your submission will be accepted and the errata are added to the list of existing errata. The existing errata can be viewed by selecting your title from http://www.packtpub.com/support.

Questions

You can contact us at questions@packtpub.com if you are having a problem with some aspect of the book, and we will do our best to address it.

1
Overview

When we say Language Integrated Query, we might think that it is already integrated into the programming language, just as we write SQL queries in our application. So what is the difference or additional features that we are going to get in LINQ? How is LINQ going to make our programming life easier? Also, I am sure that we all want to know how the new feature, LINQ, is making use of the other new features of **C# 3.0**. We'll see many of those in this book.

LINQ Architecture

Language Integrated Query is a new feature in Visual Studio 2008 that extends the query capabilities, using C# and Visual Basic. Visual Studio 2008 comes with LINQ provider assemblies that enable the use of Language Integrated Queries with different data sources such as in-memory collections, SQL relational database, ADO.NET Datasets, XML documents and other data sources.

In Visual Studio 2008, Visual C# and Visual Basic are the languages that implement the LINQ language extensions. The LINQ language extensions use the new Standard Query Operators API, which is the query language for any collection that implements `IEnumerable<T>`. It means that all collections and arrays can be queried using LINQ. The collections classes simply needs to implement `IEnumerable<T>`, to enable it for LINQ to query the collections.

The following figure shows the architecture of LINQ, which can query different data sources using different programming languages:

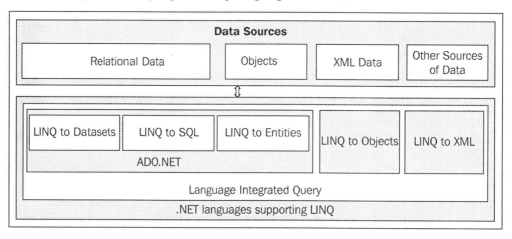

LINQ to Objects	Refers to the use of LINQ queries to access in-memory data structures. We can query any type that supports `IEnumerable(Of T)` (Visual Basic) or `IEnumerable<T>` (C#).
LINQ to SQL	LINQ to SQL is used for managing the relational data as objects. It is part of the ADO.NET family of technologies. LINQ to SQL translates the Language Integrated Queries in the object model to SQL and sends them to the database for execution. When the database returns the result, LINQ to SQL translates them back to objects that we can work with. LINQ to SQL also supports stored procedures and user-defined functions in the database.
LINQ to Datasets	LINQ to Datasets makes it easier to query the data cached in Datasets. A Dataset is disconnected, consolidated data from different data sources.
LINQ to Entities	The Entity Data Model is a conceptual data model that can be used to model the data so that applications can interact with data as entities or objects. Through the Entity Data Model, ADO.NET exposes the entities as objects.
LINQ to XML	LINQ to XML provides the in-memory document modification capabilities of the Document Object Model and supports LINQ queries. Using LINQ to XML, we can query, modify, navigate, and save the changes of an XML document. It enables us to write queries to navigate and retrieve a collection of elements and attributes. It is similar to XPath and XQuery.

Integration with SQL

LINQ to SQL supports LINQ queries against a relational database for data retrieval and manipulation. Currently in software development, we use **Relational** data for most of the applications, and we depend on database queries and objects, in some way or the other. The applications use APIs to process or get details from the database by passing queries as strings, or calling database objects by passing parameters. So what is the purpose of LINQ here? Presently scenario, we see a lot of applications, especially multi-tier applications, having a separate **data access layer** and a **business logic layer**. If we take the business logic layer, we must have lots of entities or objects to hold the information. These objects represent the database table rows in the form of objects. We use object references similar to **primary keys** in the database to identify a set of information.

To get data from a relational database to an application, the programmer ends up creating two different types of objects, but in different formats. The other disadvantage is that the programmer has to pass relational database queries as text strings from the application, then get it executed from the relational database, and pass on the information to the application objects or entity objects. We will not be able to validate the query, which is passed as text strings, until it gets compiled and executed at the database server. We cannot make use of IntelliSense or the debugging feature of the development environment to validate the queries.

Using LINQ to SQL, we can manage relational data as objects at run time using the querying facility. The LINQ queries get translated to SQL queries for the database to execute the queries, and the results are again translated to objects for the application to understand. LINQ uses the same connection and transaction features of current .NET framework for connecting to the database and manipulating the data under transaction. We can also make use of the IntelliSense feature for validating LINQ queries. To represent relational data, we need to create classes for the entities. For creating the entity classes, we need to specify some custom attributes to the class declaration. This is to make the entity objects have similar properties as that of the database objects.

Integration with XML

LINQ to XML is a new concept that supports queries against XML data. This is similar to the LINQ queries with relational data, but here the source of data is XML. Using LINQ to XML, we can manipulate XML documents and elements, create or save XML documents, and traverse through the XML tree.

When we use XML, we will be talking about elements and attributes. XML trees are composed of only attributes and elements. If we look at W3C DOM, the XML document object contains the whole XML tree in it. All elements and attributes are created within the context of the XML document. For example, the .NET 2.0 way of creating the XML element, Icecream using XML Document object model is shown below:

```
XmlDocument xdoc = new XmlDocument();
XmlElement Icecream = xdoc.CreateElement("Icecream");
```

This is an unnecessary dependency that we have to follow.

.NET 3.0 avoids creating XML document objects and we can directly create elements and attributes. For example, the following code is used for creating the Icecream element using XElement.

```
XElement Icecream = new XElement("Icreceram", "Chocolate Fudge");
```

The XML document feature is still supported for adding information like processing instructions and comments to XML.

LINQ to XML has better features than DOM for handling names and namespaces, fragments, loading XML, inner XML, annotations, and schema information.

Functional construction is a new approach taken by LINQ to XML for constructing XML elements. Using functional construction, we can create the entire XML tree in a single statement. XElement is the main class used for the construction. It has different constructors by which we can construct an XML tree. We will see this in detail later when we discuss functional construction. This is one of the important features of LINQ to XML.

LINQ to XML has a set of classes under its hierarchy structure for constructing and manipulating XML data. XElement, XNode, XName, XContainer, XAttribute and XText are some of the classes in the hierarchy. XElement is the main class for building and manipulating the XML tree.

Support for C# 3.0 Language Features

There are various features in C# 3.0 which support LINQ. They are explained in detail.

Anonymous Types

Anonymous types are used to define strong types without defining the full class. Anonymous types are strongly typed and checked at compile time. This type is widely used by LINQ, because LINQ returns dynamically-shaped data, whose type is determined by the LINQ query. In LINQ, the types are defined in situations where the types are needed temporarily, or just once. For example, given an ice-cream which has properties like name, flavor, ingredients, price, and fat content, we might sometimes only need the name of the ice-cream and the price. Anonymous type helps us to define a dynamic type containing only the name and price of the `Icecream` object. This is also called shaping the result of the data being queried into a different structure or format than the original data source.

For example, following is a class that is defined for an application, and objects created and assigned some data to it.

```
public class Icecream
{
  public string name;
  public string ingredients;
  public string totalFat;
  public string cholesterol;
  public string totalCarbohydrates;
  public string protein;
  public double price;
}

List<Icecream> icecreamsList = new List<Icecream>
{
  new Icecream
  {
    name="Chocolate Fudge Icecream",
    ingredients="cream, milk, mono and diglycerides...",
    totalFat="20g",
    cholesterol="50mg",
    totalCarbohydrates="35g",
    protein="4g",
    price=10.5
  },
  new Icecream
  {
    name="Vanilla Icecream",
    ingredients="vanilla extract, guar gum, cream...",
```

```
            totalFat="16g",
            cholesterol="65mg",
            totalCarbohydrates="26g",
            protein="4g", price=9.80
        },
        new Icecream
        {
            name="Banana Split Icecream",
            ingredients="Banana, guar gum, cream...",
            totalFat="13g",
            cholesterol="58mg",
            totalCarbohydrates="24g", protein="6g",
            price=7.5
        }
    };
```

I have created a list, containing details of different ice-creams. Now I can use the projection or transformation capabilities of LINQ, and create structure and give a custom shape to something other than the original `Icecream` object. I don't have to explicitly define a new class for the new custom shaped structure. Instead, I can use the anonymous type feature to implicitly define a new type with just two properties to represent my custom shaped data.

```
    var IcecreamsWithLessPrice =
      from ice in icecreamsList
      where ice.Price < 10
      select new
      {
        Name = ice.Name,
        Price = ice.Price
      };
    Console.WriteLine("Ice Creams with price less than 10:");
      foreach (var icecream in IcecreamsWithLessPrice)
      {
        Console.WriteLine("{0} is {1}", icecream.Name,
          icecream.Price);
      }
```

In this code, I am declaring an anonymous type within the CIT clause in my LINQ query. The anonymous type has only two properties, `Name` and `Price`, whose property names and values are inferred from the shape of the query.

In the next step, I am referring to the `IEnumerable<T>` collection of this anonymous type returned by the query and loop over them and extract the details. This feature gives it a dynamic language-like flexibility.

Object Initializers

Object initializers lets you assign values to the properties of an objects at the time of creating the object. Normally in .NET 1.1 and 2.0, we define the class with properties, then create the instance, and then define the values for properties either in constructor or in the function which is using the object. Here, in C# 3.0 we can define the values at the time of creation itself. Consider the following example of class `Icecream` with two auto-implemented properties. Auto-implemented properties are the properties without a local variable to hold the property value.

```
public class Icecream
{
   public string Name { get; set; }
   public double Price { get; set; }
}
```

Now when I create the new object of type `Icecream`, I can directly assign values directly.

```
Icecream ice = new Icecream { Name = "Chocolate Fudge
                              Icecream", Price = 11.5 };
```

This is not only for the auto-implemented properties, but I can also assign a value to any accessible field of the class. The following example has a field named `Cholestrol` added to it.

```
public class Icecream
{
public string Name { get; set; }
public double Price { get; set; }
public string Cholestrol;
}
```

Now I can assign values to this new field added to the class at the time of creating the object itself.

LINQ query expressions make use of these object initializers for initializing anonymous types. In the *Anonymous Types* section, as discussed previously, we have a `select` query which creates an anonymous type with two properties. The values are also assigned using object initializers.

```
var IcecreamsWithLessPrice =
   from ice in icecreamsList
   where ice.Price < 10
   select new
   {
     Name = ice.Name,
     Price = ice.Price
   };
```

Collection Initializers

Collection initializers use object initializers to initialize their object collection. By using a collection initializer, we do not have to initialize objects by having multiple calls. For example, in the *Anonymous Types* section a little earlier, we created a list named `icecreamsList` which is a collection of `Icecreams`. All `Icecream` objects added to the collection are initialized using the collection initializer, as follows:

```
List<Icecream> icecreamsList = new List<Icecream>
{
    new Icecream
    {
      Name="Chocolate Fudge Icecream",
      Ingredients="cream, milk, mono and diglycerides...",
      Cholesterol="50mg",
      Protein="4g",
      TotalCarbohydrates="35g",
      TotalFat="20g",
      Price=10.5
    },
    new Icecream
    {
      Name="Vanilla Icecream",
      Ingredients="vanilla extract, guar gum, cream...",
      Cholesterol="65mg",
      Protein="4g",
      TotalCarbohydrates="26g",
      TotalFat="16g",
      Price=9.80
    },
    new Icecream
    {
      Name="Banana Split Icecream",
      Ingredients="Banana, guar gum, cream...",
      Cholesterol="58mg",
      Protein="6g",
      TotalCarbohydrates="24g",
      TotalFat="13g",
      Price=7.5
    }
};
```

Partial Methods

Microsoft introduced the concept of partial classes in .NET 2.0, which allows multiple developers to work on the same class file at the same time. This feature provides a way to split the definition of a class in multiple files. All these files are combined at the time of compilation. This is very helpful in adding new code or new functionality to the class without disturbing the existing class files; partial is a keyword modifier used for splitting the class.

Partial method is a new feature introduced in .NET 3.0 which is similar to partial classes. Partial methods are a part of partial classes, where the implementer of one part of the class just defines the method, and the other implementer can implement the method. It is not necessary that the second implementer of the class has to implement the method. If the method is not implemented, the compiler removes the method signature and all the calls to this method. This helps the developer to customize the code with his own implementation. It is safe to declare the partial methods without worrying about the implementation. The compiler will take care of removing all the calls to the method. Following is an example for defining and implementing partial methods:

```
// Defining UpdateItemsList method in Items1.cs file
partial void UpdateItemsList();
//Implemeting UpdateItemsList method in Items2.cs file
partial void UpdateItemsList()
{
   // The method Implementation goes here
}
```

There are some constraints in using partial methods. They are as follows:

1. Method declaration must begin with the keyword partial and the method should return void.

2. Methods can have ref parameters, but not out parameters.

3. Methods cannot be virtual, as they are private implicitly.

4. Partial methods cannot be extern as the presence of a body determines whether they are defining or implementing.

5. We cannot make a delegate to a partial method.

Implicitly Typed Local Variables

Implicitly typing variables is a new feature that makes your job easier. The compiler takes care of identifying the type of variables from the value used for initializing the variables. LINQ also make use of this new feature for identifying the type of data that results from the LINQ queries. The programmer need not specify the return type of the querie's result. We normally declare variables by specifying the type of the variable. For example, to declare variables of type integer, string, and array of integers we would be writing it as:

```
int    iCount  =  0;
string sName = "Hi";
int[] iIntegers = new int[] {1,2,3,4,5,6,7,8,9};
```

The equivalent of the above declarations using implicit typing would be as follows:

```
var iCount = 0;
var sName = "Hi";
var iIntegers = new int[] {1,2,3,4,5,6,7,8,9};
```

We have used the keyword `var` and a value for initializing the variable. We have not used any type for the variable. In this case, the compiler takes care of defining the variable type from the value assigned to it. The variable `iCount` is considered as an integer as the value assigned to it is an integer. So for any variable to be an implicitly typed variable, it should have an initializing value assigned to it, and it cannot have null value assigned to it. As the type is defined by the initial value, the initial value cannot be changed over the lifetime of the program. If we do so, we will end up getting an error while compiling.

We can also use implicit typing for declaration of collections. This is very useful when instantiating complex generic types. For example, the normal way of declaring a collection which holds item numbers is given as follows:

```
List<int> itemNumbers = new List<int>();
itemNumbers.Add(100005);
itemNumbers.Add(100237);
itemNumbers.Add(310078);
```

The equivalent for the above declaration, using implicit typing, would be as follows:

```
var itemNumbers = new List<int>();
itemNumbers.Add(100005);
itemNumbers.Add(100237);
itemNumbers.Add(310078);
```

In all the previous cases, the implicit type declaration has some restrictions and limitations:

- We should use only the `var` keyword with an initializer for the declaration.
- The intializer cannot be a null value.
- The initializer cannot be an object or collection by itself.

Once initialized, the type cannot be changed throughout the program. Even though implicit typing gives the advantage of not specifying the type of the variable, it is better practice to use typed variable in order to clearly know the type of the variable declared.

Extensions

Extension methods are static methods that can be invoked using instance method syntax. Extension methods are declared using `this` keyword as a modifier on the first parameter of the method. Extension methods can only be declared in static classes. The following is an example of a static class that has the extension method `CountCharacters` to count the number of characters in the parameter string:

```
namespace Newfeatures.Samples
{
  public static class Example
  {
    public static int CountCharacters(string str)
    {
      var iCount = str.Length;
      return iCount ;
    }
  }
}
```

To test the above extension methods, include the following code into the main method of the program. Now run the application and test it.

```
static void Main(string[] args)
{
  string[] strings = new string[]
  {"Name", "Chocolate Fudge Icecream" };
  foreach (string value in strings)
  Console.WriteLine("{0} becomes: {1}",value,
  Example.CountCharacters(value));
}
```

In order to define the previous method to be an extension method that can be invoked using the instance method syntax, include the keyword `this` as the modifier for the first parameter:

```
public static int CountCharacters(this string str)
```

In the `Main` method, change the invocation of `CountCharacters` to use the instance method syntax making `CountCharacters` appear as a method of the string class, as shown:

```
static void Main(string[] args)
{
   string[] strings = new string[]
   { "Name", "Chocolate Fudge Icecream"};
      foreach (string value in strings)
      Console.WriteLine("{0} becomes: {1}",
      value, value.CountCharacters());
   }
```

Extension methods can also be added to generic types, such as `List<T>` and `Dictionary<T>`, as in the case of normal types.

```
public static List<T> result<T>(this List<T> firstParameter, List<T>
secondParameter)
{
   var list = new List<T>(firstParameter);
   // required coding
   return list;
}
```

It is recommended that we use extension methods only when it is really required. It is better to use inheritance, and create a new type by deriving the existing type wherever it is possible. An extension method will not be called if it has the same signature as a method defined in the type. Extension methods are defined at the `namespace` level, so we should avoid using it when we create class libraries.

Expressions

The various types of expressions used in LINQ are explained below.

Lambda Expressions

Anonymous methods in C# 2.0 help us to avoid declaring a named method by writing methods inline with code. This can be used in places where we need the functionality only within the parent method. We cannot reuse the anonymous method code in the other methods, as it is available within the parent method. Following is an example for finding a particular string from a list of strings:

```
class Program
{
    static void Main(string[] args)
    {
        List<string> icecreamList = new List<string>();
        icecreamList.Add("Chocolate Fudge Icecream");
        icecreamList.Add("Vanilla Icecream");
        icecreamList.Add("Banana Split Icecream");
        icecreamList.Add("Rum Raisin Icecream");
        string vanilla = icecreamList.Find(FindVanilla);
        Console.WriteLine(vanilla);
    }
    public static bool FindVanilla(string icecream)
    {
        return icecream.Equals("Vanilla Icecream");
    }
}
```

The equivalent anonymous method for the above code would be as follows:

```
List<string> icecreamList1 = new List<string>();
icecreamList1.Add("Chocolate Fudge Icecream");
icecreamList1.Add("Vanilla Icecream");
icecreamList1.Add("Banana Split Icecream");
icecreamList1.Add("Rum Raisin Icecream");
string vanilla1 = icecreamList1.Find(delegate(string icecream)
{
    return icecream.Equals("Vanilla Icecream");
});
Console.WriteLine(vanilla1);
```

In the previous example, a method is defined inline and we do not have any external method to find the string.

Now C# 3.0 has a new feature called lambda expression which helps us to avoid the anonymous methods itself. For example, here is the equivalent method with lambda expression for the previous anonymous method.

```
// Using Lambda Expressions
List<string> icecreamList2 = new List<string>();
icecreamList2.Add("Chocolate Fudge Icecream");
icecreamList2.Add("Vanilla Icecream");
icecreamList2.Add("Banana Split Icecream");
```

```
icecreamList2.Add("Rum Raisin Icecream");
string vanilla2 = icecreamList2.Find((string icecreamname)
=>icecreamname.Equals("Vanilla Icecream"));
Console.WriteLine(vanilla2);
```

A lambda expression is the lambda with the expression on the right side.

(input parameters separated by commas) => expression

We can also specify the types of the input paramaters; for example, `(int x, int y) => x > y`.

There is another type called statement lambda that consists of a number of statements enclosed in curly braces.

The following is an example of lambda expression with an extension method. It uses the `where` extension method to get the total number of integers, and the list of integers (which are less than 10) in the array of integers.

```
var numbers = new int[] { 1, 10, 20, 30, 40, 5, 8, 2, 9};
var total = numbers.Where(x => x < 10);
Console.WriteLine("Numbers less than ten: " + total.Count());
foreach(var val in total)
Console.WriteLine(val);
```

LINQ provides the ability to treat expressions as data at runtime using the new type `Expression<T>` which represents an expression tree. This is an in-memory representation of the lambda expression. Using this, we can modify the lambda expressions through code. By getting these expressions as data, we can also build the query statements at runtime. `System.Expressions` is the namespace used for this. There are some limitations to the lambdas. They are as follows:

- It must contain the same number of parameters as the delegate type.
- Each input parameter in the lambda must be implicitly convertible to its corresponding delegate parameter.
- The return value of the lambda must be convertible to the delegate's return type.

Query Expressions

Currently, we are actually working with two different languages when we retrieve data from the database and work with our front-end applications. One would be for front-end application development and the other is the SQL for retrieving data from the database. These SQL queries are embedded into the application code as strings, so we don't get the facility of the compiler checking the query statements in quotes.

In **C# 3.0**, we have LINQ which gives the benefit of strong type checking. Also, we don't need to depend on SQL queries and writing it within quotes. LINQ is similar to relational database queries. Query expressions provide the language integrated syntax for queries.

The query expression begins with a `from` clause and ends with a `select` or a `group` clause. The `from` clause can be followed by many `from`, `let`, or `where` clauses. The `from` clause is a generator, the `let` clause is for computing the value, the `where` clause is for filtering the result and `select` or `group` specifies the shape of the result. There are other operators like `orderby`. For example, the query below is to select ice-creams with price less than 10.

```
from Icecream Ice in Icecreams
where Ice.Price <= 10.0
select Ice
```

Following are the syntax for the query expressions:

query-expression:
   from-clause query-body

from-clause:
   `from` type$_{opt}$ `identifier` `in` `expression` `join-clauses`$_{opt}$

join-clauses:
   join-clause
   join-clauses join-clause

join-clause:
   `join` type$_{opt}$ `identifier` `in` `expression` `on` `expression` `equals` `expression`
   `join` type$_{opt}$ `identifier` `in` `expression` `on` `expression` `equals` `expression`
   `into` `identifier`

query-body:
   from-let-where-clauses$_{opt}$ `orderby-clause`$_{opt}$ `select-or-group-clause` query-continuation$_{opt}$

from-let-where-clauses:
   from-let-where-clause
   from-let-where-clauses from-let-where-clause

from-let-where-clause:
   from-clause
   let-clause
   where-clause

let-clause:
   `let` `identifier` `=` `expression`

where-clause:
```
where  boolean-expression
```

orderby-clause:
```
orderby  orderings
```

orderings:
```
ordering
orderings  ,  ordering
```

ordering:
```
expression  ordering-direction_{opt}
```

ordering-direction:
```
ascending
descending
```

select-or-group-clause:
```
select-clause
group-clause
```

select-clause:
```
select  expression
```

group-clause:
```
group  expression  by  expression
```

query-continuation:
```
into  identifier  join-clauses_{opt}  query-body
```

C# 3.0 actually translates the query expressions into invocation of methods like `where`, `select`, `orderby`, `groupby`, `thenby`, `selectmany`, `join`, `cast`, `groupjoin` that have their own signatures and result types. These methods implement the actual query for execution. The translation happens as a repeated process on the query expressions, until no further translation is possible. For example, the following query:

```
from Icecream Ice in Icecreams
where Ice.Cholestrol == "2mg"
select Ice
```

...is first translated into:

```
from Icecream Ice in Icecreams.Cast<Icecream>()
where Ice.Cholestrol == "2mg"
select Ice
```

...the final translation would be as follows:

```
Icecreams.Cast<Icecream>().Where(Ice => Ice.Cholestrol == "2mg")
```

The following query:

```
from Ice in Icecreams
group Ice.Name by Ice.Cholestrol
```

...is translated into the following:

```
Icecreams.GroupBy(Ice => Ice.Cholestrol, Ice =>Ice.Name
```

Let us see how we can make use of these queries with in-memory collections. The System.Linq namespace has all the standard query operators. We have to use this namespace for writing queries. Create a class, Icecream as follows:

```
public class Icecream
    {
       public string name;
       public string ingredients;
       public string totalFat;
       public string cholesterol;
       public string totalCarbohydrates;
       public string protein;
       public double price;
    }
```

Using the above Icecream class, create list of ice-creams and assign that to a list variable. We will see how we can easily retrieve information from this list using queries.

```
List<Icecream> icecreamsList = new List<Icecream>
{
new Icecream("Chocolate Fudge Icecream", "cream, milk, mono and
diglycerides...", "20g", "50mg", "35g", "4g", 10.5),
new Icecream ("Vanilla Icecream", "vanilla extract, guar gum,
ream...", "16g", "65mg", "26g", "4g", 9.80 ),
new Icecream ("Banana Split Icecream", "Banana, guar gum,
cream...", "13g", "58mg", "24g", "6g", 7.5)
};
```

The following query will return the name and price of the ice-creams with a price less than or equal to 10. In this query we have not specified any type for variables; it's all implicit. Even if we want to specify the type, it is not easy to identify the type of the value returned for the query.

```
var icecreamswithLeastPrice =
from Ice in icecreamsList
where Ice.price <= 10
select new { Ice.name, Ice.price };
```

```
Console.WriteLine("Icecreams with least price: ");
foreach (var ice in icecreamswithLeastPrice)
{
    Console.WriteLine(ice.name + " " + ice.price);
}
```

Let us see how we can leverage the feature of lambda expressions here. For example, we will find out the list of ice-creams with a lower price using the lambda expressions. Include the following code to the main method of the program after creation of the `icecreamsList`.

```
var count = icecreamsList3.Count<Icecream>(Ice => Ice.price <=0);
Console.WriteLine("Number of Icecreams with price
less than ten: {0} ", count);
```

The above lambda expression will return the total number of ice-creams with a price less than or equal to 10.

Expression Trees

Expression trees are an in-memory representation of a lambda expression. Using this we can modify and inspect the lambda expressions at runtime using expression trees in the `System.Linq.Expressions` namespace. Lambda expressions are compiled as code or data, depending on the context they are used in. If we assign a lambda expression to a variable of type `delegate`, then the compiler will generate the corresponding executable code; but we assign the lambda expression to a variable of the generic type `Expression<T>`, so the compiler won't create the executable code, but will generate an in-memory tree of objects that represents the structure of the expression. These structures are known as expression trees.

For example, consider the following lambda expression using delegate:

```
Func<int, int> func = x => x + 5;
```

This code is compiled as executable and can be executed as follows:

```
var three = func(1);
```

The same delegate is no longer compiled as executable, but compiled as data if we define the delegate as expression tree:

```
Expression<Func<int, int>> expression = func => x + 5;
```

To use this expression in the application, it has to be compiled and invoked as follows:

```
var originalDelegate = expression.Compile();
var three = originalDelegate.Invoke(2);
```

Each node in the expression tree represents an expression. If we decompose the expression, we can find out how the expression tree represents the lambda expressions. Following is the sample code to decompose the previous expression:

```
ParameterExpression parameter =
ParameterExpression)expression.Parameters[0];
BinaryExpression operation = (BinaryExpression)expression.Body;
ParameterExpression left = (ParameterExpression)operation.Left;
ConstantExpression right = (ConstantExpression)operation.Right;

Console.WriteLine("Decomposed expression: {0} => {1} {2} {3}",
parameter.Name, left.Name, operation.NodeType, right.Value);
```

The output of the above decomposition would be:

```
Decomposed expression: func => func Add 5
```

Expression trees are implemented in the `System.Query.dll` assembly under the `System.Linq.Expressions` namespace. The abstract class `Expression` provides the root of a class hierarchy used to model expression trees. The `Expression` class contains static factory methods to create expression tree nodes of various types.

There are many different abstract classes used to represent the different types of elements in an expression. These classes are derived from the non-generic version of `Expression`. The following table examines some abstract classes derived from the `Expression` class.

Class	Description	Parameters
lambda expression	This is the bridge between the generic `Expression<T>` class and non-generic `Expression` class.	Its main properties are body and parameters. Body—represents the body of the expression. Parameters—represents the list of parameters it uses.
constant expression	This represents the constant values that appear in the expression.	Value is it's main property, which returns the constant value in the expression.
parameter expression	Represents a named parameter expression. Values must be passed to parameter to evaluate the expression.	Name is the property of the parameter expression to represent the name of the parameter.
unary expression	Represents an expression that has the unary operator.	The main property of this class is operand which is associated with the operand in expression.

Class	Description	Parameters
binary operator	This is to represent the binary operators, like sum, multiplication, and many others.	The main properties of this class are left and right which provides access to the left and right operand in the expression.
method call expression	This represents the method call in an expression.	The main properties of this class are: Method — metadata information associated to the method to be called. Object — the object to which the method call will be applied. Parameters — to represent the arguments used in the method.
conditional expression	Represents an expression that has a conditional operator.	The main properties of conditional expression are. `IfFalse` — gets the expression to execute if the test evaluates to false. `IfTrue` — gets the expression to execute if the test evaluates to true.

Summary

In this chapter, we have seen an overview of Language Integrated Query. The architecture diagram explains the different types of LINQ which are used for querying data from different sources of data. Also, we have seen some of the new features of C# 3.0 and above in relation to LINQ. This chapter also explained some of the new features introduced in C# 3.5 such as partial methods, expressions and anonymous types with some examples for each of those. We will be looking into details of LINQ features and its usability in the coming chapters.

2
LINQ to Objects

LINQ to Objects means that we can use LINQ to query objects in a collection. We can access the in-memory data structures using LINQ. We can query any type of object that implements the `IEnumerable` interface or `IEnumerable<T>`, which is of generic type. Lists, arrays, and dictionaries are some collection objects that can be queried using LINQ. If we don't use LINQ, we have to use the looping method to filter the values in a collection. We have to go through the values one-by-one and then find the required details. However, using LINQ we can directly query collections and filter the required values without using any looping. LINQ provides powerful filtering, ordering, and grouping capabilities that requires minimum coding. For example, if we want to find out the types stored in an assembly and then filter the required details, we can use LINQ to query the assembly details using `System.Reflection` classes. The `System.Reflection` namespace contains types that retrieve information about assemblies, modules, members, parameters, and other entities as collections are managed code, by examining their metadata. Also, files under a directory are a collection of objects that can be queried using LINQ. We shall see some of the examples for querying some collections.

Array of Integers

The following example shows an integer array that contains a set of integers. We can apply the LINQ queries on the array to fetch the required values.

```
int[] integers = { 1, 6, 2, 27, 10, 33, 12, 8, 14, 5 };
  IEnumerable<int> twoDigits =
  from numbers in integers
  where numbers >= 10
  select numbers;
  Console.WriteLine("Integers > 10:");
  foreach (var number in twoDigits)
  {
    Console.WriteLine(number);
  }
```

The `integers` variable contains an array of integers with different values. The variable `twoDigits`, which is of type `IEnumerable`, holds the query. To get the actual result, the query has to be executed.

The actual query execution happens when the query variable is iterated through the `foreach` loop by calling `GetEnumerator()` to enumerate the result. Any variable of type `IEnumerable<T>`, can be enumerated using the `foreach` construct. Types that support `IEnumerable<T>` or a derived interface such as the generic `IQueryable<T>`, are called queryable types. All collections such as list, dictionary and other classes are queryable. There are some non-generic `IEnumerable` collections like `ArrayList` that can also be queried using LINQ. For that, we have to explicitly declare the type of the range variable to the specific type of the objects in the collection, as it is explained in the examples later in this chapter.

The `twoDigits` variable will hold the query to fetch the values that are greater than or equal to 10. This is used for fetching the numbers one-by-one from the array. The `foreach` loop will execute the query and then loop through the values retrieved from the integer array, and write it to the console. This is an easy way of getting the required values from the collection.

If we want only the first four values from a collection, we can apply the `Take()` query operator on the collection object. Following is an example which takes the first four integers from the collection. The four integers in the resultant collection are displayed using the `foreach` method.

```
IEnumerable<int> firstFourNumbers = integers.Take(4);
Console.WriteLine("First 4 numbers:");
foreach (var num in firstFourNumbers)
{
   Console.WriteLine(num);
}
```

The opposite of `Take()` operator is `Skip()` operator, which is used to skip the number of items in the collection and retrieve the rest. The following example skips the first four items in the list and retrieves the remaining.

```
IEnumerable<int> skipFirstFourNumbers = integers.Skip(4);
Console.WriteLine("Skip first 4 numbers:");
foreach (var num in skipFirstFourNumbers)
{
   Console.WriteLine(num);
}
```

This example shows the way to take or skip the specified number of items from the collection. So what if we want to skip or take the items until we find a match in the list? We have operators to get this. They are `TakeWhile()` and `SkipWhile()`.

For example, the following code shows how to get the list of numbers from the `integers` collection until 50 is found. `TakeWhile()` uses an expression to include the elements in the collection as long as the condition is true and it ignores the other elements in the list. This expression represents the condition to test the elements in the collection for the match.

```
int[] integers = { 1, 9, 5, 3, 7, 2, 11, 23, 50, 41, 6, 8 };
IEnumerable<int> takeWhileNumber = integers.TakeWhile(num =>
  num.CompareTo(50) != 0);
Console.WriteLine("Take while number equals 50");
foreach (int num in takeWhileNumber)
  {
    Console.WriteLine(num.ToString());
  }
```

Similarly, we can skip the items in the collection using `SkipWhile()`. It uses an expression to bypass the elements in the collection as long as the condition is true. This expression is used to evaluate the condition for each element in the list. The output of the expression is boolean. If the expression returns false, the remaining elements in the collections are returned and the expression will not be executed for the other elements. The first occurrence of the return value as false will stop the expression for the other elements and returns the remaining elements. These operators will provide better results if used against ordered lists as the expression is ignored for the other elements once the first match is found.

```
IEnumerable<int> skipWhileNumber = integers.SkipWhile(num =>
  num.CompareTo(50) != 0);
Console.WriteLine("Skip while number equals 50");
foreach (int num in skipWhileNumber)
  {
    Console.WriteLine(num.ToString());
  }
```

Collection of Objects

In this section we will see how we can query a custom built objects collection. Let us take the `Icecream` object, and build the collection, then we can query the collection. This `Icecream` class in the following code contains different properties such as `Name`, `Ingredients`, `TotalFat`, and `Cholesterol`.

```
public class Icecream
{
  public string Name { get; set; }
  public string Ingredients { get; set; }
  public string TotalFat { get; set; }
  public string Cholesterol { get; set; }
  public string TotalCarbohydrates { get; set; }
  public string Protein { get; set; }
  public double Price { get; set; }
}
```

Now build the `Icecreams` list collection using the class defined perviously.

```
List<Icecream> icecreamsList = new List<Icecream>
{
  new Icecream {Name="Chocolate Fudge Icecream", Ingredients="cream,
    milk, mono and diglycerides...", Cholesterol="50mg",
    Protein="4g", TotalCarbohydrates="35g", TotalFat="20g",
    Price=10.5
},
  new Icecream {Name="Vanilla Icecream", Ingredients="vanilla extract,
    guar gum, cream...", Cholesterol="65mg", Protein="4g",
    TotalCarbohydrates="26g", TotalFat="16g", Price=9.80 },
  new Icecream {Name="Banana Split Icecream", Ingredients="Banana, guar
  gum, cream...", Cholesterol="58mg", Protein="6g",
    TotalCarbohydrates="24g", TotalFat="13g", Price=7.5 }
};
```

We have `icecreamsList` collection which contains three objects with values of the `Icecream` type. Now let us say we have to retrieve all the ice-creams that cost less. We can use a looping method, where we have to look at the price value of each object in the list one-by-one and then retrieve the objects that have less value for the `Price` property. Using LINQ, we can avoid looping through all the objects and its properties to find the required ones. We can use LINQ queries to find this out easily. Following is a query that fetches the ice-creams with low prices from the collection. The query uses the `where` condition, to do this. This is similar to relational database queries. The query gets executed when the variable of type `IEnumerable` is enumerated when referred to in the `foreach` loop.

```
List<Icecream> Icecreams = CreateIcecreamsList();
IEnumerable<Icecream> IcecreamsWithLessPrice =
from ice in Icecreams
where ice.Price < 10
select ice;
```

```
Console.WriteLine("Ice Creams with price less than 10:");
foreach (Icecream ice in IcecreamsWithLessPrice)
{
   Console.WriteLine("{0} is {1}", ice.Name, ice.Price);
}
```

As we used `List<Icecream>` objects, we can also use `ArrayList` to hold the objects, and a LINQ query can be used to retrieve the specific objects from the collection according to our need. For example, following is the code to add the same `Icecreams` objects to the `ArrayList`, as we did in the previous example.

```
ArrayList arrListIcecreams = new ArrayList();
arrListIcecreams.Add( new Icecream {Name="Chocolate Fudge Icecream",
   Ingredients="cream, milk, mono and diglycerides...",
   Cholesterol="50mg", Protein="4g", TotalCarbohydrates="35g",
   TotalFat="20g", Price=10.5 });
arrListIcecreams.Add( new Icecream {Name="Vanilla Icecream",
   Ingredients="vanilla extract, guar gum, cream...",
   Cholesterol="65mg", Protein="4g", TotalCarbohydrates="26g",
   TotalFat="16g", Price=9.80 });
arrListIcecreams.Add( new Icecream {Name="Banana Split Icecream",
   Ingredients="Banana, guar gum, cream...", Cholesterol="58mg",
   Protein="6g", TotalCarbohydrates="24g", TotalFat="13g", Price=7.5
});
```

Following is the query to fetch low priced ice-creams from the list.

```
var queryIcecreanList = from Icecream icecream in arrListIcecreams
where icecream.Price < 10
select icecream;
```

Use the `foreach` loop, shown as follows, to display the price of the objects retrieved using the above query.

```
foreach (Icecream ice in queryIcecreanList)
Console.WriteLine("Icecream Price : " + ice.Price);
```

Reading from Strings

We all know that a string is a collection of characters. It means that we can directly query a string value. Now let us take a string value and try to find out the number of upper case letters in the string. For example, assign a string value to the variable `aString` as shown below.

```
string aString = "Satheesh Kumar";
```

Now let us build a query to read the string and find out the number of characters that are in upper case. The query should be of type `IEnumerable`.

```
IEnumerable<char> query =
from ch in aString
where Char.IsUpper(ch)
select ch;
```

The query uses the `Char.IsUpper` method in the `where` clause to find out the upper case letters from the string. The following code displays the number of characters that are in upper case:

```
Console.WriteLine("Count = {0}", count);
```

Reading from Text Files

A file could be called a collection, irrespective of the data contained in it. Let us create a text file that contains a collection of strings. To get the values from the text file, we can use LINQ queries. Create a text file that contains names of different ice-creams. We can use the `StreamReader` object to read each line from the text file. Create a `List` object, which is of type `string`, to hold the values read from the text file. Once we get the values loaded into the strings `List`, we can easily query the list using LINQ queries as we do with normal collection objects. The following sample code reads the text file, and loads the ice-cream names to the string list:

```
List<string> IcecreamNames = new List<string>();
using( StreamReader sReader = new StreamReader(@"C:\Icecreams.txt"))
{
  string str;
  str = sReader.ReadLine();
  while (str != null)
  {
    IcecreamNames.Add(str);
  }
}
```

The following sample code reads the list of strings and retrieves the name of ice-creams in descending order:

```
IEnumerable<string> icecreamQuery =
from name in IcecreamNames
orderby name descending
select name;
```

We can verify the result of the query by displaying the names using the following code:

```
foreach (string nam in icecreamQuery)
{
   Console.WriteLine(nam);
}
```

The following code displays the names and verifies the result of the query:

```
foreach (string nam in icecreamQuery)
{
   Console.WriteLine(nam);
}
```

Similar to collections used in above examples, the .NET reflection class library can be used to read metadata of the .NET assembly and create the types, type members, parameters, and other properties as collections. These collections support the IEnumerable interface, which helps us to query using LINQ.

LINQ has lot of standard query operators which can be used for querying different objects that support IEnumerable interface. We can use all standard query operators, listed in the following table, against objects.

Query Operator type	Query Operators
Restriction	Where, OfType
Projection	Select, SelectMany
Joining	Join, GroupJoin
Concatenation	Concat
Sorting	OrderBy, OrderByDescending, ThenBy, ThenByDescending, Reverse
Set	Distinct, Except, Intersect, Union
Grouping	GroupBy
Conversion	AsEnumerable, Cast, OfType, ToArray, ToDictionary, ToList, ToLookup
Equality	SequenceEqual
Element	DefaultIfEmpty, ElementAt, ElementAtOrDefault, First, FirstOrDefault, Last, LastOrDefault, Single, SingleOrDefault
Generation	Empty, Range, Repeat
Quantifiers	All, Any, Contains
Aggregation	Aggregate, Average, Count, LongCount, Max, Min, Sum
Partitioning	Skip, SkipWhile, Take, Takewhile

Summary

In this chapter, we saw some examples to query different objects using LINQ operators. We can use LINQ queries on any object that supports `IEnumerable`. By using LINQ, we can avoid using looping methods to loop through the collections and fetch the required details. LINQ provides powerful filtering, ordering, and grouping methods. This will reduce our coding as well as the development time.

3
LINQ to XML

LINQ to XML is a new in-memory XML programming API to work against XML data. There are different ways of creating XML trees in .NET. LINQ to XML is the new method of creating and manipulating XML data through .NET. The properties and methods of LINQ help us to navigate and manipulate the XML elements and attributes.

LINQ uses a feature called functional construction for creating the XML tree. The .NET compiler translates XML literals into calls to the equivalent XML constructor to build the objects. LINQ to XML also provides the object model for creating and manipulating the XML data. This feature also integrates well in the .NET framework. The namespaces which supports LINQ and LINQ to XML are as follows:

```
using System.Linq;
using System.Xml.Linq;
```

The namespaces have changed from the May CTP. We need to include these namespaces into our project to take advantage of the LINQ to XML features. There are a lot of XML-specific query operators that come with LINQ, which we can use for querying and manipulating the XML elements and values, as we do in our normal SQL queries. Visual Studio also provides IntelliSense for accessing some of the query methods and properties that will make a developer's life easier.

In this chapter, we will see how to use LINQ to XML features for navigating and manipulating the XML elements and attributes.

Features

Using LINQ queries, we can query data from different sources, whether it is relational or XML. LINQ to XML is the XML programming language built on the .NET Language Integrated Query framework. Using LINQ to XML we can create, update, and delete XML elements in the XML tree. It also provides streaming, and the transformation and querying feature, similar to XQuery and XPath.

XQuery is a language which can query structured or semi-structured XML data. XQuery is based on the XPath language. It has the ability to iterate, sort, and construct the necessary XML. If the XML document is stored in the SQL server database, which has support for XML, the document can be queried using XQuery. The result of the XQuery can be typed or un-typed. The type information of the result is based on the type, which is specified in the XML schema language.

LINQ provides query features to write queries against XML, as we do normally with the relational data model. LINQ provides different query operators, such as projections, aggregates, partitioning, grouping, and conversion.

The developers can take advantage of writing LINQ queries instead of writing normal SQL queries, to reduce their coding work and get high performance. We can take advantage of .NET 3.5 features, as LINQ and LINQ to XML are integrated in the .NET framework. If we are using LINQ with Visual Studio, we can also use IntelliSense and statement completion feature provided by Visual Studio for easy programming.

The results of the queries from LINQ, and LINQ to XML, are strongly typed. This increases the robustness of the application. All the errors are caught at compile time instead of runtime, as it happens when we write SQL queries while programming.

Technical architects or software designers, can design their own LINQ providers for the data source they use. By implementing a new provider, they can give the query, language support to the data model they use. They can also take advantage of using some of the features of the .NET 3.0 framework.

Class Library

All the classes of LINQ to XML are present in the System.Xml.Linq namespace; we have seen most of the LINQ to XML classes in the examples given in the previous sections. Following is the list of LINQ to XML classes present in the System.Xml. Linq namespace and the hierarchy of classes.

Classes and Hierarchy

The major high level classes defined in LINQ to XML are as follows:

- XName
- XNamespace
- XNode
- XDeclaration
- XAttribute
- XObject

The XNode class has the second level of classes, listed as follows:

- XText
- XComment
- XContainer
- XDocumentType
- XProcessingInstruction

The XContainer has two more classes further down as:

- XElement
- XDocument

Below is the diagrammatic representation of classes defined in LINQ to XML:

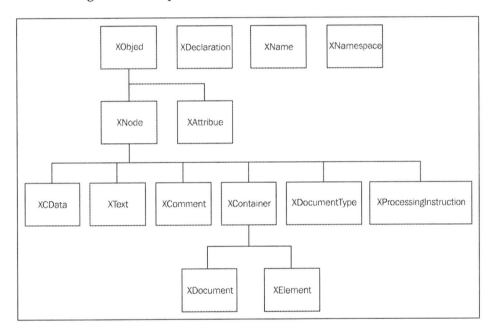

We will see details of the important classes used, to work with the elements and attributes in XML documents, in the following sections.

XElement Class

This is one of the fundamental classes of all LINQ to XML classes. The entire XML tree is created using this class, as we have seen in the functional construction section. XML data manipulation and traversing through the XML tree happens using `XElement` object, as seen in the following code:

```
new XElement("Nutrition","Calories:290",
new XAttribute("TotalFat", "18g"))
```

XAttribute Class

These are the name or value pair associated with an XML element, but they are not derived from nodes. Working with attributes is similar to working with `XElements`. Using functional construction, attributes are added to the elements to form the XML tree. The `XAttribute` class has one constructor which takes two parameters. The first parameter specifies the name, and the second specifies the content, as shown in the following code:

```
new XElement("Nutrition","Calories:290",
new Xattribute("TotalFat", "18g"))
```

XDocument Class

Similar to W3C DOM, the `XDocument` is a container for the XML document. The `XDocument` can contain one root `XElement`, `XComment`, `XDeclaration`, and `XProcessingInstruction`. For example:

```
XmlDocument Icecreams = new XmlDocument();
```

Other Classes

An `XNode` represents any item that is represented as a node in the XML tree. `XElements`, `XComments` and `XDocument`, `XDocumentType`, and `XProcessingInstructions` and `XText` are some of the nodes represented in the XML tree.

The `XComments` class is used for adding comments to the XML. `XProcessingInstruction` is for providing additional information to the application that processes the XML data.

Following is the code for adding some of the nodes to the XML:

```
// Adding Declaration, Comments and PI
  XDocument IcecreamsDocument = new XDocument
  (
     new XDeclaration("1", "utf-8", "yes"),
     new XComment("XML data Manipulation using LINQ"),
     new XProcessingInstruction("Instructions", "12345-67890"),
     new XElement("Icecreams",
       new XElement("Icecream",
         new XElement("Name", "Chocolate Fudge Icecream"),
         new XElement("Ingredients", "cream, milk, sugar, corn syrup,
         cellulose gum, mono and diglycerides..."),
         new XElement("Cholesterol", "50mg"),
         new XElement("TotalCarbohydrates", "35g"),
         new XElement("Protein","4g")
     )
   )
 );
```

Here we have the XDocument object, IcecreamsDocument, which has a declaration, comment, and processing instruction added to it. XElement is used for creating the nodes of the XML document. The output for the above code will be as follows:

```
<?xml version="1.0" encoding="utf-8" standalone="yes"?>
<!--XML data Manipulation using LINQ-->
<?Instructions 12345-67890?>
<Icecreams>
  <Icecream>
    <Name>Chocolate Fudge Icecream</Name>
    <Ingredients>cream, milk, sugar, corn syrup, cellulose gum, mono
    and diglycerides...</Ingredients>
    <Cholesterol>50mg</Cholesterol>
    <TotalCarbohydrates>35g</TotalCarbohydrates>
    <Protein>4g</Protein>
  </Icecream>
</Icecreams>
```

LINQ to XML with Other XML Technologies

When we talk about using XML, the first thing that comes to our mind is the XML DOM. We use XML programming API of W3C Document Object Model (DOM). XML programming means either traversing or manipulating data in the XML tree. These are the only things that we normally do with an XML document. In case of XML DOM, we follow the "bottom-up" approach of creating the XML document using `XmlDocument` object first and then building the XML elements and attributes. We do programming with elements and attributes. Coming up is an example of creating an XML document using XML DOM, which is the standard way of doing it using ADO.NET 2.0.

The following code creates an XML document `Icecreams` to store different varieties of ice-creams as XML elements. Each ice-cream element contains many elements to hold the properties of ice-cream. Each XML element is created separately and then added to the main `Icecream` element as children. After adding all the properties as elements, the main `Icecream` element itself is added to the document as an XML element. Like this, we can keep on adding the elements to the document and build the XML tree.

```
XmlDocument Icecreams = new XmlDocument();
XmlElement Name = Icecreams.CreateElement("Name");
Name.InnerText = "Chocolate Fudge Icecream";
XmlElement Ingredients =
Icecreams.CreateElement("Ingredients");
Ingredients.InnerText = "cream, milk, sugar, corn syrup,
                         cellulose gum, mono and diglycerides...";
XmlElement SaturatedFat = Icecreams.CreateElement("SaturatedFat");
SaturatedFat.SetAttribute("type", "SaturatedFat");
SaturatedFat.InnerText = "20g";
XmlElement TransFat = Icecreams.CreateElement("TransFat");
TransFat.SetAttribute("type", "TransFat");
TransFat.InnerText = "5g";
XmlElement OtherFat = Icecreams.CreateElement("OtherFat");
OtherFat.SetAttribute("type", "OtherFat");
OtherFat.InnerText = "10g";
XmlElement Cholesterol = Icecreams.CreateElement("Cholesterol");
Cholesterol.InnerText = "50mg";
XmlElement TotalCarbohydrates =
                        Icecreams.CreateElement("TotalCarbohydrates");
TotalCarbohydrates.InnerText = "35g";
XmlElement Protein = Icecreams.CreateElement("Protein");
```

```
Protein.InnerText = "4g";
XmlElement Icecream = Icecreams.CreateElement("Icecream");
Icecream.AppendChild(Name);
Icecream.AppendChild(Ingredients);
Icecream.AppendChild(SaturatedFat);
Icecream.AppendChild(TransFat);
Icecream.AppendChild(OtherFat);
Icecream.AppendChild(TotalCarbohydrates);
Icecream.AppendChild(Protein);
Icecreams.AppendChild(Icecream);
Icecreams.Save(@"C:\Icecreams.XML");
```

LINQ to XML simplifies this XML document creation process. We don't need to create the XML Document object to create elements and attributes of the XML tree. Using LINQ, we can create the XML tree directly using the XElement object. Here is how we can construct the same code as seen previously, using LINQ:

```
XElement IceCreams =
new XElement("Icecreams",
    new XElement("Icecream",
    new XElement("Name", "Chocolate Fudge Icecream"),
    new XElement("Ingredients", "cream, milk, sugar, corn
        syrup, cellulose gum, mono and diglycerides..."),
    new XElement("TotalFat", "20g",
        new XAttribute("SaturatedFat", "8g"),
        new XAttribute("TransFat", "12g")),
    new XElement("Cholesterol", "50mg"),
    new XElement("TotalCarbohydrates", "35g"),
    new XElement("Protein","4g")
)
);
IceCreams.Save(@"C:\Icecreams2.XML");
```

In the example, we don't see an XmlDocument object for creating the XML tree. This is the main advantage of .NET 3.5. In W3C DOM, everything happens in the context of the document object; we can directly use the XElement object for creating elements and attributes and we can even save this to a file. We don't need to depend on the XmlDocument object. Following is the code for loading an XML document using the W3C DOM.

```
XmlDocument DOMLoadIcecreams = new XmlDocument();
DOMLoadIcecreams.Load(@"C:\Icecreams.xml");
```

The equivalent code would be:

```
XElement LoadIcecreams = XElement.Load(@"c:\Icecreams.xml");
```

XElement is the main object used for loading the XML as well as saving the XML. The XmlDocument object is nowhere in the picture when we use LINQ.

Following is a list of features that differentiates LINQ from W3C DOM. Most of the features are well supported by LINQ.

Feature	Support by LINQ
Namespaces	LINQ to XML provides a better approach for namespaces than DOM. An XML name consists of an XML namespace, which is also called XML namespace URI. XML namespace is similar to the namespace used in .NET Framework and the purpose is the same. It helps us uniquely identify elements and attributes in the XML document without having any name conflicts in different parts of the XML document.
DTD Constructs	LINQ to XML does not support `XmlEntityReferences`. When an XML tree is populated, all DTD entities are expanded. This simplifies the XML construction.
XPath	LINQ to XML does not support `Xpath` queries. Instead we can use LINQ features.
XmlDocumentFragment	LINQ to XML does not support `XmlDocumentFragment` class. It is handled by the query result, which is of the `IEnumerable<XNode>` type.
XPathNavigator	No support.
BaseURI	No support. LINQ to XML does not store any URI information.
InnerXml	LINQ to XML provides a read only XML property which returns the InnerXml and also through `Parse` method. DOM provides support for getting and setting InnerXML.
Annotations	LINQ to XML elements support an extensible set of annotations, whereas the `XmlElement` does not support this. This is useful to add additional information to the element.
Schema Information	LINQ to XML nodes are extensible via annotations. LINQ to XML does not provide any schema information.

LINQ with XmlReader

LINQ to XML is implemented on top of the XmlReader, but each of these is used for different purposes.

XmlReader provides a fast-forward only, and non-cached access to XML data. It can be used in places where we have to navigate through a large amount of XML data without any manipulations. XmlReader will be helpful performance-wise, but will not be able to update the data as it returns read only data.

If we have to deal with different sources of data involving data manipulation, we can go for LINQ to XML, as it provides an in-memory XML programming.

LINQ with XSLT

XSLT (Extensible Stylesheet Language Transformation) is the definition language for XML data presentation and transformations. XSLT is derived from the XSL (Extensible Stylesheet Language). The presentation gives a specific format or style to the XML document, and transformation, reading the nodes of the XML tree, and converting that to the required tree.

XSLT and LINQ to XML are two different approaches for getting the XML transformations. Both are flexible and powerful ways of doing the transformation.

In case of XSLT, it is an independent programming language, which is rule based and has a declarative approach. XSLT is used in situations where multiple web applications have the same transformation style, but possibly have different sources of data. Performance wise, it helps a lot but the disadvantage is that the developers cannot make use of the C# or VB.NET. programming language The developer has to depend on these two different programming languages, which is a complex process. Also, it is difficult to maintain.

LINQ to XML provides the feature of functional construction, by which we can construct the XML objects dynamically, by pulling the data from different sources. Constructing transformation is very easy, which helps the user not to depend on other programming language, like XSLT. This reduces a lot of maintenance and development work.

LINQ with MSXML

MSXML can be used from any programming language that supports COM. MSXML is a COM-based technology for processing XML. MSXML provides a native implementation of the DOM with support for XSLT and XPath. It is not recommended for use in managed code, based on the Common Language Runtime (CLR)

Functional Construction

Functional construction is how we construct the XML tree. Using LINQ, we can construct the entire XML tree with only the XElement class. XElement has three constructors for constructing the XML tree:

1. XElement(XName name) — creates an XML element with the name specified in the XName parameter.

2. XElement(XName name, object content) — creates an element with the name specified in the XName parameter, and the content passed in by the object content.

3. XElement(XName name, params object[] content) — creates an element with the name specified in the XName parameter, and the second parameter is the child element created by the paremeter list. It could be any valid object, which can be a child of an element. It can be another XElement or an XAttribute or any of the following:

- A string, which is added as text content. This is the recommended pattern to add a string as the value of an element; the LINQ implementation will create the internal XText node.

- An XText, which can be a string or CData value, added as child content. This is mainly useful for CData values; using a string is simpler for ordinary string values.

- An XElement, which can be added as a child element.

- An XAttribute, which can be added as an attribute.

- An XProcessingInstruction or XComment, which is added as child content.

- An IEnumerable, which is enumerated, and these rules are applied recursively.

- null, which is ignored.

Let us see how we can build an XML tree using the functional construction method. The code for building an XML tree, which has details of Icecream, is as follows:

```
Icecreams.Add(
    new XElement("Icecream",
    new XElement("Name", "Vanilla Icecream"),
    new XElement("Ingredients", "vanilla extract,
        guar gum, cream, nonfat milk, sugar,
        locust bean gum, carrageenan,
        annatto color..."),
    new XElement("Cholesterol", "65mg"),
    new XElement("TotalCarbohydrates", "26g"),
    new XElement("Protein", "4g",
        new XAttribute("Vitamin A","1g"),
        new XAttribute("Calcium", "2g"),
        new XAttribute("Iron", "1g")),
    new XElement("TotalFat", "16g",
        new XAttribute("SaturatedFat","7g"),
        new XAttribute("TransFat", "9g"))
    )
);
```

The first `XElement` object, `Icecreams`, uses the following constructor:

```
XElement(XName name, params object[] content)
```

The second parameter takes the number of `XElement` objects as content. This will be the child of this parent element that gets created. The child element in turn can have any number of `XElements`. So the `Icecreams` element has the child element `Icecream`, which in turn has many elements such as `Name`, `Ingredients`, `Cholesterol`, and `TotalCarbohydrates`.

The `XElement` name is constructed with the use of the constructor:

```
XElement(XName name, object content)
```

This takes the `XName` for the name of the element and content for the element. This element is added as one of the child elements for the `Icecream` element:

```
new XElement("Name", "Vanilla Icecream")
```

The output of this will be as follows:

```
<Name>Vanilla Icecream</Name>
```

If we have to create an element with only the `XName`, and without the content, we can use the following constructor:

```
XElement(XName name)
```

For example, , `XElement Icecream = new XElement("Icecream")`, will give output:

```
<Icecream/>
```

Let us save this `XElement` using the **Save** method and see the XML tree created by the functional construction using `XElement`.

```
Icecreams.Save(@"C:\Icecreams");
```

The output of the above created `XElement Icecream` would be:

```
<?xml version="1.0" encoding="utf-8"?>
<Icecreams>
  <Icecream>
    <Name>Vanilla Icecream</Name>
    <Ingredients>vanilla extract, guar gum, cream, nonfat milk,
                sugar, locust bean gum, carrageenan,
                annatto color...
    </Ingredients>
    <Cholesterol>65mg</Cholesterol>
```

```
    <TotalCarbohydrates>26g</TotalCarbohydrates>
    <Protein VitaminA="1g" Calcium="2g" Iron="1g">4g</Protein>
    <TotalFat SaturatedFat="7g" TransFat="9g">16g</TotalFat>
  </IcecreamTwo>
</Icecreams>
```

To create the above XML file, we have used only the functional construction feature of LINQ.

XML Names

An XML name consists of an XML namespace, which is also called XML namespace URI. XML namespace is similar to the namespace used in .NET framework and the purpose is the same. It helps us uniquely identify the elements and attributes in the XML document, without having any name conflicts in different parts of the XML document. The XML names are represented by an XNamespace object and a local name. For example, if you want to create an element Icecreams, you might want to create it under a namespace called http://yourcompany.com/Icecreams.

To make the XML document more understandable, we can use a prefix for the namespaces. Prefixes allow us to create a shortcut for an XML namespace. LINQ simplifies this by introducing the XNamespace object and a local name. So when reading in XML, each XML prefix is resolved to its corresponding XML namespace. The class that represents XML names is XName, which consists of XNamespace and a local name. The code below is an example of defining the namespace and using it in the node:

```
XNamespace nspace = "http://yourcompany.com/Icecreams/";
XElement Icecreamss = new
XElement("{http://yourcompany.com}IcecreamsList");
```

The string representation of an XName is referred to as an expanded name. An expanded name looks like this:

```
{NamespaceURI}LocalName
```

Instead of constructing a namespace object, we can use the expanded name, but we need to type the namespace every time we need the XName. To avoid this, we can take advantage of the language feature of defining the namespace and use it with the local name:

```
XNamespace nspace = "http://yourcompany.com/";
XElement Icecreamss = new
XElement("{http://yourcompany.com}IcecreamsList",
```

```
        new XElement(nspace + "Icecream",
        new XElement(nspace + "Name",
                     "Rum Raisin Icecream"),
        new XElement(nspace + "Ingredients", "Rum, guar
                     gum, nonfat milk, cream, alomnds,
                     sugar, raisins, honey, chocolate,
                     annatto color..."),
        new XElement(nspace + "Protein", "6g",
            new XAttribute("Iron", "4g")),
        new XElement(nspace + "TotalCarbohydrates", "28g")
    )
    );
Icecreamss.Save(@"c:\Icecreamss.xml");
```

The previous example has one expanded name used with the `Icecreamss` element. All other elements use the namespace defined as `nspace`. It is not that the entire node should be part of the same namespace. They can be different from one another. For example, change the namespace value `nspace` to `http://yourcompany.com/Icecream/`, and see the difference in namespace value for the elements. It will be as follows:

```
<?xml version="1.0" encoding="utf-8"?>
<IcecreamsList xmlns="http://yourcompany.com">
  <Icecream xmlns="http://yourcompany.com/Icecream">
    <Name>Rum Raisin Icecream</Name>
    <Ingredients>Rum, guar gum, nonfat milk, cream, alomnds, sugar,
                 raisins, honey, chocolate, annatto color...
    </Ingredients>
    <Protein Iron="4g">6g</Protein>
    <TotalCarbohydrates>28g</TotalCarbohydrates>
  </Icecream>
</IcecreamsList>
```

Loading and Traversing XML

Now that we've seen how to create a basic XML tree and the basic classes of LINQ to XML and its hierarchy, let's take a more detailed look at loading XML data and finding our way through it.

Loading XML

There are different ways of loading XML data. The XML data can be in the form of a file, or a string, or any other supported formats. Using LINQ to XML, we can load XML data through the XElement object. For example, to load XML data from a file, we can use the Load method of the XElement object, as given below:

```
// Loading XML
    XElement LoadIcecreams = XElement.Load(@"c:\Icecreams.xml");
```

If the XML data is in the form of a string, we can load it through XElement by using the Parse method. For example, the code for loading Icecreams from string is as follows:

```
XElement LoadIcecreamsfromString = XElement.Parse(
    @"<Icecream>
        <Name>Rum Raisin Icecream</Name>
        <Cholesterol>49mg</Cholesterol>
        <VitaminA type=""VitaminA"">2g</VitaminA>
        <VitaminC type=""VitaminC"">1g</VitaminC>
        <Iron type=""Iron"">4g</Iron>
        <TotalCarbohydrates>email@xyz.com</TotalCarbohydrates>
    </Icecream>");
```

Traversing XML

In this section, we will see how we can walk through the XML tree, which is also called traversing through XML. There are several methods provided by LINQ to get all the children of the XElement.

Nodes() is the method used mainly for traversing. This returns the IEnumerable<object> because the XML can have a different type and it also gives the sequential access to items in the collection. For example, let us have the following XML file called Icecreams.xml.

```
<?xml version="1.0" encoding="utf-8"?>
<Icecreams>
  <Icecream>
    <Name>Chocolate Fudge Icecream</Name>
    <Ingredients>cream, milk, sugar, corn syrup, cellulose gum, mono
    and diglycerides...</Ingredients>
    <Cholesterol>50mg</Cholesterol>
    <TotalCarbohydrates>35g</TotalCarbohydrates>
    <Protein VitaminA="3g" Iron="1g" Calcium="3g">5g</Protein>
    <TotalFat SaturatedFat="9g" TransFat="11g">20g</TotalFat>
  </Icecream>
<!-- This is the text added at the bottom of the XML file -->
</Icecreams>
```

Load this `Icecreams.xml` file into an `XElement` object, and then using `Nodes()` method, we will traverse through the XML to get the details. The following code returns the node values from the XML file:

```
// Loading XML
    XElement LoadClassicIcecreamsFile =
    XElement.Load(@"C:\LoadClassicIcecreams.xml");
    // Traversing XML
    foreach (XNode nod in LoadClassicIcecreamsFile.Nodes())
    {
        Console.WriteLine(nod.ToString());
    }
```

The previous code gives the following output:

```
<?xml version="1.0" encoding="utf-8"?>
<Icecreams>
  <Icecream>
    <Name>Chocolate Fudge Icecream</Name>
    <Ingredients>cream, milk, sugar, corn syrup, cellulose gum, mono
                and diglycerides...</Ingredients>
    <Cholesterol>50mg</Cholesterol>
    <TotalCarbohydrates>35g</TotalCarbohydrates>
    <Protein VitaminA="3g" Iron="1g" Calcium="3g">5g</Protein>
    <TotalFat SaturatedFat="9g" TransFat="11g">20g</TotalFat>
  </Icecream>
<!-- This is the text added at the bottom of the XML file -->
</Icecreams>
```

The code outputs all element values and the text added to the XML document at the bottom. We can also filter the nodes using the name and type. For example, the following code will bring only the nodes of the `XElement` type and displays the XML value:

```
foreach (XNode nod in
        LoadClassicIcecreamsFile.Nodes()
        OfType<XElement>())
{
    Console.WriteLine(nod.ToString());
}
```

The equivalent of the above code is as follows:

```
foreach (XElement nod in
        LoadClassicIcecreamsFile.Elements())
{
    Console.WriteLine(nod.Value);
}
```

We can also get a particular element based on the name. We can use the overloaded method `Elements (XName)`, which takes `XName` as parameter. For example, the following code is used for getting the `Name` element of the `icecreams.xml` file.

```
foreach (XElement nod in LoadClassicIcecreamsFile.
Elements("Icecream"))
{
    Console.WriteLine(nod.Element("Name").Value);
}
```

If the `XElement` node has more than one child element, we can use the `Elements` method to traverse through the child elements. If we have only one child element, we can directly point to that using the `Element` method. In the above code we are looping through the `Icecreams` element as it has many children. Inside the loop, we have directly used the `Element` method to get the `Name` element from the tree as there is no child element for the `Name`. Following are some more examples of traversing through the XML and getting information about the nodes:

```
foreach (XElement node in
        LoadClassicIcecreamsFile.Elements("Icecreams"))
{
    // Value of Protein element
    Console.WriteLine("Protein : " +
                    node.Element("Protein").Value + "\n");
    // Parent to Parent of Protein element
    Console.WriteLine("GrandParent of Protein Element : "
                    + node.Element("Protein").
                    Parent.Parent.Name.ToString() + "\n");
    // Type of Protein Element
    Console.WriteLine("Protein : " + node.Element("protein")
                    .NodeType.ToString() + "\n");
    // Next node to Last Name node
    Console.WriteLine("Next node after Protein : " +
                    node.Element("Protein")
                    .NextNode.ToString() + "\n");
    // Last node in the Icecream
    Console.WriteLine(@"Last node in the Icecream element
                    : " + node.LastNode.ToString() + "\n");
    // Value of the type attribute in teh Phone element
    Console.WriteLine("Value of the type attribute in the
                    TotalFat Element : " + node.Element("TotalFat")
                    .Attribute("SaturatedFat")
                    .Value.ToString() + "\n");
    // Are there any attributes to the Employee element
    Console.WriteLine("Icecream Element has any attributes : " +
                    node.HasAttributes.ToString() + "\n");
    }
```

In the above example, we have many child elements under the `Icecreams` element. If we have to get all the elements after a particular element, or before a particular element, then we can use `ElementsAfterSelf` and `ElementsBeforeSelf` methods. For example, following is the code to get all elements after the `Name` element and all elements before the `Protein` element under the `Icecreams` element:

```
// Using ElementsAfterSelf()
string afterName = "";
string beforeProtein = "";
IEnumerable<XElement> elementsAfterName =
  IcecreamsDocument.Element("Icecreams")
.Element("Icecream").Element("Name").ElementsAfterSelf();
foreach (XElement ele in elementsAfterName)
{
  afterName = afterName + ele.Value;
}
// Using ElementsBeforeSelf()
IEnumerable<XElement> elementsBeforeProtein =
  IcecreamsDocument.Element("Icecreams")
.Element("Icecream").Element("Protein")
.ElementsBeforeSelf();
foreach (XElement eleBefore in elementsBeforeProtein)
{
  beforeProtein = beforeProtein + eleBefore.Value;
}
```

The return value of `ElementsAfterSelf()` is of the type `IEnumerable` by which we can enumerate over the elements that are siblings to this node and appear after this node in terms of XML order. The final output of the `afterName` string will have information of all elements after the `Name` element:

```
<Ingredients>cream, milk, sugar, corn syrup, cellulose gum, mono
and diglycerides...</Ingredients><Cholesterol>50mg</Cholesterol><T
otalCarbohydrates>35g</TotalCarbohydrates><Protein>4g</Protein>
```

The final output of the `beforeProtein` string will have the following information of all elements before the `Protein` element.

```
<Name>Chocolate Fudge Icecream</Name><Ingredients>cream, milk, sugar,
corn syrup, cellulose gum, mono and diglycerides...</Ingredients><Chol
esterol>50mg</Cholesterol><TotalCarbohydrates>35g</TotalCarbohydrates>
```

Data Manipulation

Data manipulation is one of the most important steps in the application development. Whether we deal with the relational data or XML data, we do some kind of data manipulation for keeping the information up-to-date. Normally, we **insert**, **update**, and **delete** the information. LINQ to XML provides a lot of features and methods for XML data manipulation. As we know XElement plays an important role in LINQ as it has many methods to add, remove, or update a node in the XML tree. We should take care of handling the NullreferenceExceptions that occur when we try to manipulate an element which does not exist in the XML document.

Inserting or Adding Elements to XML

Let's use the following code to create the XML file, with the details of an ice-cream. It consists of the ice-cream's name, dietary information, and ingredients.

```
XDocument IcecreamsDocument =  new XDocument(
            new XDeclaration("1", "utf-8", "yes"),
            new XComment("XML data Manipulation using LINQ"),
            new XProcessingInstruction
            ("Instructions", "12345-67890"),
                new XElement("Icecreams",
                  new XElement("Icecream",
                  new XElement("Name", "Chocolate Fudge
                                            Icecream"),
                  new XElement("Ingredients", "cream, milk,
                            sugar, corn syrup, cellulose
                            gum, mono and diglycerides..."),
                  new XElement("Cholesterol", "50mg"),
                  new XElement("TotalCarbohydrates", "35g"),
                  new XElement("Protein","4g")
                  )
                  )
        );
```

We will save the XML file using the Save method of the XElement object IcecreamsDocument.Save(@"C:\IcecreamsDocument.XML"); and this would produce the following XML file:

```
<?xml version="1.0" encoding="utf-8" standalone="yes"?>
<!--XML data Manipulation using LINQ-->
<?Instructions 12345-67890?>
<Icecreams>
  <Icecream>
    <Name>Chocolate Fudge Icecream</Name>
```

```
<Ingredients>cream, milk, sugar, corn syrup, cellulose gum, mono
                and diglycerides...</Ingredients>
<Cholesterol>50mg</Cholesterol>
<TotalCarbohydrates>35g</TotalCarbohydrates>
<Protein>4g</Protein>
    </Icecream>
</Icecreams>
```

Let us see how we can include new elements to the above given `Icecream` element. We can do this by calling the `Add` method of the `XElement`, and pass the new element information as a child to the `Icecream` element. The first step is to create the new `XElements` such as `Calcium`, `Iron`, and `VitaminA`.

```
XElement Calcium = new XElement("Calcium", "7g");
XElement Iron = new XElement("Iron", "6g");
XElement VitaminA = new XElement("VitaminA", "3g");
```

Then we need to add these elements to the existing elements in the `Icecreams` element. This step adds the `Calcium` content of ice-cream as the new element to the `Icecream` element, which is in the `Icecreams` element, which in turn is inside the `IcecreamsDocument` document. The `Calcium` element will be added as the last element to the `Icecream` element.

```
IcecreamsDocument.Element("Icecreams")
.Element("Icecream").Add(Calcium);
```

Now, let us add the next element, `Iron` content of ice-cream to the `Icecream` element, but we shall not add this at the end of the `Icecream` element, but just before the `Calcium` element. We need to use the `AddBeforeSelf` method on the `Calcium` element by passing the `Iron` element as parameter.

```
IcecreamsDocument.Element("Icecreams").Element("Icecream").
Element("Calcium").AddBeforeSelf(Iron);
```

We have added the `Iron` and `Calcium` elements to the `Icecream` element. This time we have to add the `VitaminA` content of `Icecream` as an element after the `Calcium` element, so that the elements will be in order. Just like we called the `AddBeforeSelf` method to the `Clacium` element, we have to call the `AddAfterSelf` method on the `Calcium` element and pass the `VitaminA` element as parameter, so that it will get added after the `Calcium` element.

```
IcecreamsDocument.Element("Icecreams").Element("Icecream").Element
("Calcium").AddAfterSelf(VitaminA);
```

After adding all the above elements, the resultant XML would be as follows:

```
<?xml version="1.0" encoding="utf-8" standalone="yes"?>
<!--XML data Manipulation using LINQ-->
<?Instructions 12345-67890?>
<Icecreams>
  <Icecream>
    <Name>Chocolate Fudge Icecream</Name>
    <Ingredients>cream, milk, sugar, corn syrup, cellulose gum, mono
                and diglycerides...</Ingredients>
    <Cholesterol>50mg</Cholesterol>
    <TotalCarbohydrates>35g</TotalCarbohydrates>
    <Protein>4g</Protein>
    <Iron>6g</Iron>
    <Calcium>7g</Calcium>
    <VitaminA>3g</VitaminA>
  </Icecream>
</Icecreams>
```

In the previous examples, we have one `Icecream` element present in the XML. If we have to add details of one more ice-cream to the above XML, we can create a new `XElement`, which contains the new ice-cream details, and then add it to the main element `IcecreamsDocument`. For example, let us create a new element of type `Icecream` with the following details:

```
XElement NewIcecreamtoAdd = new XElement("NewIcecream",
                new XElement("Name", "Vanilla Icecream"),
                new XElement("Ingredients", "vanilla extract,
                            guar gum, cream, nonfat milk,
                            sugar,locust bean gum, carrageenan,
                            annatto color..."),
                new XElement("Cholesterol", "65mg"),
                new XElement("TotalCarbohydrates", "26g"),
                new XElement("Protein", "4g",
                    new XAttribute("VitaminA", "1g"),
                    new XAttribute("Calcium", "2g"),
                    new XAttribute("Iron", "1g")),
                    new XElement("TotalFat", "16g",
                    new XAttribute("SaturatedFat", "7g"),
                    new XAttribute("TransFat", "9g"))
            );
```

Add the previous element to the `IcecreamsDocument` document as:

```
IcecreamsDocument.Element("Icecreams").Add(NewIcecreamtoAdd);
```

Now the resulting XML will contain both the ice-creams details as shown below:

```
<?xml version="1.0" encoding="utf-8" standalone="yes"?>
<!--XML data Manipulation using LINQ-->
<?Instructions 12345-67890?>
<Icecreams>
  <Icecream>
    <Name>Chocolate Fudge Icecream</Name>
    <Ingredients>cream, milk, sugar, corn syrup, cellulose gum, mono
                 and diglycerides...</Ingredients>
    <Cholesterol>50mg</Cholesterol>
    <TotalCarbohydrates>35g</TotalCarbohydrates>
    <Protein>4g</Protein>
    <Iron>6g</Iron>
    <Calcium>7g</Calcium>
    <VitaminA>3g</VitaminA>
  </Icecream>
  <NewIcecream>
    <Name>Vanilla Icecream</Name>
    <Ingredients>vanilla extract, guar gum, cream, nonfat milk,
                 sugar, locust bean gum, carrageenan, annatto
                 color...</Ingredients>
    <Cholesterol>65mg</Cholesterol>
    <TotalCarbohydrates>26g</TotalCarbohydrates>
    <Protein VitaminA="1g" Calcium="2g" Iron="1g">4g</Protein>
    <TotalFat SaturatedFat="7g" TransFat="9g">16g</TotalFat>
  </NewIcecream>
</Icecreams>
```

In all the examples that we have examined until now, for adding or inserting new elements to the exisiting XML, we saw the way in which it succeeds every time. But what if we do not have the parent element to which we are adding the new element? For example, let us try to add the element `Iron` before the element `VitaminE`, which does not exist in our XML example, above.

```
IcecreamsDocument.Element("Icecreams").Element("Icecream")
.Element("VitaminE").AddBeforeSelf(Iron);
```

LINQ will try to find the element `VitaminE` in the XML; if not found, a `NullReferenceException` will be thrown. So we need to take care of handling the `NullRefernceException`.

Inserting or Adding XML Attributes

Adding attributes is similar to adding elements to the XML tree. We can use the same functional construction to add attributes. Let us take some different XML data, instead of the same ice-creams we saw in the previous example. Let us take different varieties of ice-creams. We can add new attributes to the elements using the same functional construction method we used for adding elements. The code given below shows an example of adding attributes to the elements using functional construction. We will add the `VitaminA` attribute with value `2g`, `Iron` attribute with value `1g` to the `Protein` element. Similarly, we also have two attributes under the element `TotalFat`. All these attributes are added at the time of adding elements.

```
XElement ClassicIcecreams =
            new XElement("Icecreams",
                new XElement("IcecreamOne",
                new XElement("Name", "Chocolate Fudge Icecream"),
                new XElement("Ingredients", "cream, milk, sugar,
                            corn syrup, cellulose gum..."),
                new XElement("Cholesterol", "50mg"),
                new XElement("TotalCarbohydrates", "35g"),
                new XElement("Protein",
                    new XAttribute("VitaminA","3g"),
                    new XAttribute("Iron", "1g")),
                new XElement("TotalFat",
                    new XAttribute("SaturatedFat","9g"),
                    new XAttribute("TransFat", "11g"))
            )
            );
```

Suppose we wanted to add a new attribute to an existing element in an existing XML document. There is another method of adding attributes to the XML nodes. We can create the attribute objects and then add it to the elements, as follows:

```
XAttribute attrTyp = new XAttribute("Calcium", "1g");
ClassicIcecreams.Element("IcecreamOne")
.Element("Protein").Add(attrTyp);
```

Or we can also add the attribute, as follows:

```
ClassicIcecreams.Element("IcecreamOne").Element("Protein")
.Add(new XAttribute("Calcium", "1g"));
```

It is not guaranteed that we will always add attributes to the correct elements. Sometimes, we may make the mistake of adding attributes to an element which does not exists in the XML document. In the next example, I will try to add the `Calcium` attribute to the `TotalProtein` element, which does not exist in our XML document.

```
ClassicIcecreams.Element("IcecreamOne").Element("TotalProtein")
.Add(new XAttribute("Calcium", "1g"));
```

When the code is executed, we will get an exception of type `NullReferenceException`. So we need to take care of these exceptions when we manipulate the data in the XML document.

Deleting XML

We have seen inserting the XML elements and attributes. We should also be able to delete the existing elements and attributes. Let us say we have two more ice-creams added to the above `ClassicIcecreams` XML document, which we saw earlier. We will see how to delete the `IcecreamTwo` element from the `ClassicIcecreams` XML document.

```
//Deleting Elements
ClassicIcecreams.Element("IcecreamTwo").Remove();
```

We can use the `Remove` method of the element to remove a particular element. If we want to remove all elements under a particular element, we can use `RemoveAll()`

```
ClassicIcecreams.Element("IcecreamTwo").RemoveAll();
```

The above code will remove all the elements under the `IceCreamTwo` element, but not the `IcecreamTwo` element.

We can also use `RemoveContent()` and `RemoveAnnotation()` to remove the content and annotations from the XML.

Even if we delete elements, we should take care of the `NullreferenceExceptions` that will occur when we try to remove an element which does not exists in the XML document.

Updating XML

LINQ provides many different ways to update the existing XML data. We can use the following methods to update the elements and element values. We can change the value of an element by using the `Value` property of the `Element` object, as shown below:

```
ClassicIcecreams.Element("IcecreamTwo")
.Element("Cholesterol").Value = "69mg";
```

Or we can also use `SetElement` method to change the value of the element as follows:

```
ClassicIcecreams.Element("IcecreamOne")
.SetElementValue("Protein", "5g");
```

We can also create a new `XElement` and then replace that with the one that exists in the XML document. For example:

```
XElement prc = new XElement("TotalCarbohydrates", "28mg");
ClassicIcecreams.Element("IcecreamTwo").ReplaceWith(prc);
```

The entire name of the element can also be changed using the `Name` property, as follows:

```
ClassicIcecreams.Element("IcecreamOne").Name = "Icecream1";
```

Deleting XML Attributes

Similar to deleting the XML element, we can delete the attributes using the `Remove` method of the attribute object.

```
//Deleting attributes
ClassicIcecreams.Element("IcecreamOne").Element("Protein").
Attribute("Calcium").Remove();
```

In the previous statement, the `Calcium` attribute for the `Protein` element in the `IcecreamOne` element is removed by calling the `Remove` method.

Attributes can also be removed by using the `RemoveAttributes` method of an element, which will remove all the attributes under that element. The following example will remove all the attributes under the `Protein` element, which is under the `IcecreamOne` element.

```
ClassicIcecreams.Element("IcecreamOne").Element("Protein")
.RemoveAttributes();
```

Updating XML Attributes

Similar to updating the XML element, we can update the properties of the XML attributes. For example, the code below shows the method of updating the value `Calcium` attribute under the element `Protein`.

```
//Setting Attribute value
ClassicIcecreams.Element("IcecreamOne").Element("Protein")
.Attribute("Calcium").Value = "2g";
```

The following code is the equivalent of the previous code with a different value:

```
ClassicIcecreams.Element("IcecreamOne").Element("Protein")
.SetAttributeValue("Calcium", "3g");
```

Outputting and Streaming XML

For saving XML details in a file, we can directly use the `Save` method of `XElement` by passing the name of the file in which the XML has to be stored. The `Save` method requires the file parameter. To save the `Icecreams` XML tree created earlier in a file, we can use the following method, which saves the XML tree data to the `C:\Icecreams.xml` file.

```
ClassicIcecreams.Save(@"C:\IceCreams.XML");
```

We can also use the `XmlWriter` for outputting the XML data into a file. For example, following is the code which writes the XML tree after the `Icecreamone` element within the `Icecreams` element.

```
XmlWriterSettings settings = new XmlWriterSettings();
settings.OmitXmlDeclaration = true;
settings.ConformanceLevel = ConformanceLevel.Auto;
settings.CloseOutput = false;
// Write out the Icecreamone node tree
XmlWriter writer = XmlWriter.Create(@"C:\Ice.xml",
                                     settings);
ClassicIcecreams.Element("IcecreamOne").WriteContentTo(writer);
writer.Flush();
writer.Close();
```

First we need to create the `XmlWriter` object that points to the XML file in which we have to store the XML data. If required, we can change the settings for the writer according to your needs. We need to use the `WriteContentTo` method on the element from which we want the XML data to be sent to the writer. The name of the writer object is passed as parameter to the `WriteContentTo` method.

Streaming XML

XML streaming is very useful when serializing objects. For example, let us say we have an array of instances of object of type `Icecream`. Let us see how we can serialize some of the objects to XML.

```
IcecreamList[] ListofIcecreams;
```

LINQ to XML provides `XStreamingElement` for serializing the elements directly instead of creating the tree and then serializing it. If we use use `XElement` in the case of `StreamingElement`, it will create the `XElement` tree and iteraten through the elements. The process of creating the tree and iterating through the elements is eliminated by using `XStreamingElement`. Each `XStreamingElement` saves itself to the output stream. But if you see the end result, it will be the same in the cases of `XElement` and `XStreamingElement`.

Create the class, `IcecreamList`, as shown below:

```
class IcecreamList
{
  public string flavor;
  public string servingSize;
  public double price;
  public string nutrition;
  public IcecreamList(string flv, string srvS, double prc,
                      string nut)
  {
      flavor = flv;
      servingSize = srvS;
      price = prc;
      nutrition = nut;
  }
};
```

Now declare an array of object of type `IcecreamList` class and initialize.

```
IcecreamList[] ListofIcecreams = new IcecreamList[2];

        ListofIcecreams[0] = new IcecreamList("Vanilla", "Half
                                Cup", 11, "Calories:250");
        ListofIcecreams[1] = new IcecreamList("Strawberry", "Half
                                Cup", 15, "Calories:230");
```

Now using the `XStreamingElement`, serialize the objects to XML and then save it to a file.

```
XStreamingElement str =
   new XStreamingElement("ListofIcecreams",
   from cre in ListofIcecreams
   select new XStreamingElement("Icecream",
     new XStreamingElement("Flavor", cre.flavor),
        new XStreamingElement("Price", cre.price)
     ));
   str.Save(@"C:\streamFile.xml");
```

Querying XML

Querying is a very important feature of LINQ when compared to the other XML technologies. We might have used and written a lot of SQL queries to manipulate and use the relational data. LINQ gives us the feature of querying XML. LINQ provides different operators that are similar to the SQL queries. We will see more details about the query operators in Chapter 7. LINQ provides the feature of querying details from different data models in a single query. We will see some of those through examples in the following sections.

In LINQ, methods can also be called to perform some operations. The query operators are the methods which can be operated on any object that implements the `IEnumerable<T>` class. This way of calling query methods can be referred to as **Explicit Dot Notation**.

Query Operators

We have different types of operators that we can use in LINQ on XML. We will be seeing more of these operators in Chapter 7. In that chapter, we will see the details of classifications and what each one of these classifications mean and the usage of each operator. Here we will see how we can make use of these operators against XML data. These operators are classified as follows:

- Projection operators
- Partitioning operators
- Join operators
- Grouping operators
- Conversion operators
- Aggregate operators

Out of all these operators, there are a few operators which are common for all queries. They are `where`, `select`, `OrderBy`, `GroupBy`, and `SelectMany`.

We will see more about each one of these operators in detail, with examples in Chapter 7, *Standard Query Operators*.

Queries

Let us take an example of new XML data that has details of different ice-creams.

```
XElement Icecreams =
    new XElement("Icecreams",
    new XElement("Icecream",
    new XComment("Cherry Vanilla Icecream"),
    new XElement("Flavor", "Cherry Vanilla"),
    new XElement("ServingSize", "Half Cup"),
    new XElement("Price", 10),
    new XElement("Nutrition",
        new XElement("TotalFat", "15g"),
        new XElement("Cholesterol", "100mg"),
        new XElement("Sugars","22g"),
        new XElement("Carbohydrate", "23g"),
        new XElement("SaturatedFat", "9g"))));
    Icecreams.Add(
    new XElement("Icecream",
    new XComment("Strawberry Icecream"),
    new XElement("Flavor", "Strawberry"),
    new XElement("ServingSize", "Half Cup"),
    new XElement("Price", 10),
    new XElement("Nutrition",
        new XElement("TotalFat", "16g"),
        new XElement("Cholesterol", "95mg"),
        new XElement("Sugars","22g"),
        new XElement("Carbohydrate", "23g"),
        new XElement("SaturatedFat", "10g"))));
```

In the above XML, we have the details of two different ice-creams. Add some more ice-creams' details for better understandable results of the following queries. All of the operators that we use in queries are defined under the `System.Linq` namespace.

We will build a query to fetch ice-creams from the above list that have a price value equal to 10. We will also display the results by giving the flavours in order, and all the names in uppercase letters. Following is the query to get the result using the `where`, `select`, and `OrderBy` operators. We have also used the direct method

`ToUpper()` to change all the letters to uppercase. The result will contain a list of ice-creams, ordered according to the flavour, as the `Orderby` operator is used against the element `Flavour`.

```
XElement IcecreamsList = new XElement("IcecreamsList",
(from c in Icecreams.Elements("Icecream")
where (c.Element("Price").Value == "10")
orderby c.Element("Flavour").Value select new XElement("Icecream",
    c.Element("Flavour").Value.ToUpper()))));
```

Let us assume the above query returns ten records. Now, if I would like to take records from second to fifth in order, leaving the other records, we would have to make use of the `Skip()` and `Take()` operators. The following code, shows how we can apply these operators in the above query.

```
XElement NewIcecreamList = new XElement("IcecreamsList",
(from c in Icecreams.Elements("Icecream")
where (c.Element("Price").Value == "10")
orderby c.Element("Flavour").Value
select new XElement("Icecream",
    c.Element("Flavour").Value.ToUpper().Skip(1).Take(4))));
```

The query operators are the methods that can be operated on any objects that implement `IEnumerable<T>` class. We will see how we can create an object, make it `IEnumerable`, and use query operators to query the XML.

First, we'll create the class and include variables corresponding to the elements in the XML. We'll create a constructor to initialize all the variables of the class.

```
class NewIcecreamList
{
public string flavor;
public string servingSize;
public double price;
public string nutrition;
public IcecreamList(string flv, string srvS,
                    double prc, string nut)
{
    flavor = flv;
    servingSize = srvS;
    price = prc;
    nutrition = nut;
}
};
```

After creating the class, we construct a query using the above class. The query should hold the list of ice-creams, and their details. It should be of the type `IEnumerable<IcecreamList>`.

```
// Simple Query
IEnumerable<IcecreamList> IcrmList =
from c in Icecreams.Elements()
select new IcecreamList(
(string)c.Element("Flavor"),
(string)c.Element("ServingSize"),
(double)c.Element("Price"),
(string)c.Element("Nutrition")
);
```

We retrieve details of ice-creams from the `IcrmList` variable, which is of type `IEnumerable<IcecreamList>`, and display that in a rich text box, which is added in the form. This code will give a list of ice-creams with details such as `Flavour`, `ServingSize`, `Price`, and `Nutrition`.

```
foreach (IcecreamList p in IcrmList)
Console.WriteLine(p.flavor + ":" + p.servingSize +
          ":" + p.price + ":" + p.nutrition + "\n");
```

If we don't have values for any element in the XML, how do we handle it? For example, in the previous XML data, the `Nutrition` value is missing and whenever the `Nutrition` value is empty we should display null in that. In this case, the query would be as follows:

```
XElement Icecreams2 = new XElement("Icecreams2",
from c in Icecreams.Elements("Icecream")
select new XElement("Icecream",
(string)c.Element("Flavor"),
(string)c.Element("ServingSize"),
(string)c.Element("Price"),
c.Elements("Nutrition").Any() ?
    new XElement("Nutrition", c.Elements("Nutrition").ToString()):null
    )
);
```

The `Any()` operator is used here to check if the element is empty, or whether there is any value in it. If the element is not empty then return the null value. If it is present, return the element which is similar to `Nutrition` with the same name.

Ancestors and Descendants

These are the methods to get particular element's ancestors and the descendants in the XML tree structure. We can get this for any element, whatever its level may be. The first line is to get the `TotalFat` element from the `Icecreams` tree. Using the `Ancestors` methods, we can get the ancestors of the `TotalFat` element.

```
XElement Totalfat = Icecreams.Descendants("TotalFat").First();
foreach (XElement ele in Totalfat.Ancestors())
{
   Console.WriteLine(ele.Name.LocalName);
   Console.WriteLine("\n");
}
```

Similar to `Ancestors`, we can also get the list of elements which are descendant to a particular element in an XML tree. In the above examples, we have seen a lot of descendants to the `Icecreams` element and also we have many descendants to the `Nutrition` element. Using the following code, we can retrieve the descendant elements of the `Nutrition` element in the XML tree.

```
XElement Nutrition = Icecreams.Descendants("Nutrition").First();
foreach (XElement ele in Nutrition.Descendants())
{
   Console.WriteLine(ele.Name.LocalName);
}
```

The ancestors and descendants are a very interesting feature, which helps us to retrieve a particular type of elements from the XML tree. For example, in our XML tree, we have different types of ice-creams. Let us say the customer wants to know all the flavours available. In that case, we can use a simple query to list the ice-cream flavours available, shown in the following code:

```
IEnumerable<string> strList =
from flv in Icecreams.Descendants("Flavor")
select (string)flv;
foreach ( string val in strList)
{
   Console.WriteLine(val + " \n");
}
```

The list will have values like *Cherry Vanilla* and *Strawberry*.

XML Transformation

The most common way of transforming XML in any programming language is to use XSLT. In the case of LINQ to XML, the functional construction plays a major role in transforming the XML data. We can easily build the XML tree by fetching details from other XML or sources of data. We will take the `Icecream` list example used in the `Queries` section. The `Icecreams` list has details of ice-creams such as `Flavour`, `ServingSize`, `Price`, and `Nutrition`; with `Nutrition` having many elements in it. Using these details, let's say we want to build another list only having the flavour and the nutrition details, and let's call the list `IcecreamsNutritionDetails`. Let us see how we can build this using the functional construction and using the `Icecreams` XML.

```
XElement IcecreamsNutritionDetails =
                            new XElement("IcecreamsNutritionDetails",
    from c in Icecreams.Elements("Icecream")
    orderby c.Element("Flavor").Value
    select new XElement("Icecream",
        c.Element("Flavor"),
        c.Element("Nutrition"))));
```

This query builds the `IcecreamsNutritionDetails` list using the details in `Icecreams` XML. We only extracted details like `Flavour` and `Nutrition`. In the above example, the `IcecreamsNutritionDetails` element is root of the XML, which holds element details. The next element in the XML tree is the `Icecream` element, which holds details of individual ice-cream items.

In the above example, the query fetches details from the other XML for constructing a new XML. There could be a possibility that the same details might be required in another part of the application. Not only that; we might need more readability to the code that we write. In this case, we can make use of functions in the queries. We have to break up the query and move part of the query to a function. This will also break the complex query into simpler functions. Let us break the above query as follows:

```
XElement IcecreamsNutritionDetails =
                            new XElement("IcecreamsNutritionDetails",
    GetIcecreamsNutritionDetails(Icecreams));
```

Here the root element is the same, but the construction part is moved to a function called `GetIcecreamsNutritionDetails` and is used in the query. Following is the function which constructs the elements using the `Icecreams` XML.

```
public IEnumerable<XElement> GetIcecreamsNutritionDetails(
                        XElement Icecreams)
{
```

```
        return from c in Icecreams.Elements("Icecream")
        orderby c.Element("Flavor").Value
        select new XElement("Icecream",
             c.Element("Flavor"),
             c.Element("Nutrition"));
}
```

The return type of the function is IEnumerable of type XElement. We can break down the queries to any level depending on its complexity.

Dictionaries

Dictonaries in .NET represents a generic collection of key/value pairs. Each element in a dictionary is a key/value pair where the key is the unique identifier.

Convert Dictionary to XML

It is possible to convert this kind of data structure to XML, and XML as back to a different data structure. In this section, we will see some examples of converting dictionaries to XML and XML to dictionaries.

Below is the code sample of a new dictionary that holds names of four different varieties of ice-creams.

```
// Create a new Dictionary and add different types of Icecreams
    Dictionary<string, string> dictIcecream =
        new Dictionary<string, string>();
    dictIcecream.Add("Icecream1", "Cherry Vanilla Icecream");
    dictIcecream.Add("Icecream2", "Strawberry Icecream");
    dictIcecream.Add("Icecream3", "Chocolate Fudge Icecream");
    dictIcecream.Add("Icecream4", "Banana Split Icecream");
```

Using LINQ we can retrieve information from the dictionary and construct an XML. For example, following is a query that fetches information from the above dictionary and constructs an XML tree. The key in the key/value pair of the dictionary is used as the name of the XML element, and the value in the key/value pair is used as the XML element value. The value is taken from the dictionary using the key.

```
// Create XML using XElement and get details from the above dictionary
XElement Icecreams = new XElement("Icecreams",
    from key in dictIcecream.Keys
    select new XElement(key, dictIcecream[key])
);
```

The `Icecream` element will have the full XML details fetched by the query. Now the following code displays the `Icecream` element:

```
// display the details of the Icecreams elements
Console.WriteLine(Icecreams.ToString());
```

When the above code is executed, the output will be the following XML:

```
<Icecreams>
  <Icecream1>Cherry Vanilla Icecream</Icecream1>
  <Icecream2>Strawberry Icecream</Icecream2>
  <Icecream3>Chocolate Fudge Icecream</Icecream3>
  <Icecream4>Banana Split Icecream</Icecream4>
</Icecreams>
```

Create Dictionary from XML

In the previous section, we have seen the construction of XML using dictionary data. In this section we will see how we can create a dictionary from the XML data. Following is the code that creates the XML element, containing four different ice-cream varieties.

```
// XML element containing different Icecreams
    XElement Icecreams = new XElement("Icecreams",
        new XElement("Icecream1", "Cherry Vanilla Icecream"),
        new XElement("Icecream2", "Strawberry Icecream"),
        new XElement("Icecream3", "Chocolate Fudge Icecream"),
        new XElement("Icecream4", "Banana Split Icecream")
    );
```

The following code creates a dictionary to hold the values.

```
// Create a new dictionary
Dictionary<string, string> dictIcecreams =
    new Dictionary<string, string>();
```

Now retrieve all the element details from the `Icecream` element and add them to the dictionary one-by-one. The name of the element will be the key, and the value of the element will be the value of the key in the dictionary.

```
// Retrieving the detail from the above XElement and add it to the
    dictionary foreach (XElement ele in Icecreams.Elements())
    dictIcecreams.Add(ele.Name.LocalName, ele.Value);
```

Now loop through the dictionary according to the number of keys in the dictionary and display their details.

```
// Get the details from dictionary and display it to view
foreach (string str in dictIcecreams.Keys)
    Console.WriteLine(str + ": " + dictIcecreams[str]);
```

The output of the above code will be as follows:

```
Icecream1: Cherry Vanilla Icecream
Icecream2: Strawberry Icecream
Icecream3: Chocolate Fudge Icecream
Icecream4: Banana Split Icecream
```

Writing XML as Text Files and CSV Files

As we saw in the previous section, we can convert XML to a different data structure and different data structure to XML. For example, the following code creates an XML tree with `Icecreams` as the root element:

```
// Create XML Tree using XElement
    XElement ClassicIcecreams =
        new XElement("Icecreams",
        new XElement("Icecream",
        new XElement("Name", "Chocolate Fudge Icecream"),
        new XElement("Cholesterol", "50mg"),
        new XElement("TotalCarbohydrates", "35g"),
        new XElement("Protein",
            new XAttribute("VitaminA", "3g"),
            new XAttribute("Iron", "1g")),
        new XElement("TotalFat",
        new XAttribute("SaturatedFat", "9g"),
        new XAttribute("TransFat", "11g"))
    ) );
    // Add new type of Icecream to the existing XML
    ClassicIcecreams.Add(
            new XElement("Icecream",
            new XElement("Name", "Vanilla Icecream"),
            new XElement("Cholesterol", "65mg"),
            new XElement("TotalCarbohydrates", "26g"),
            new XElement("Protein", "4g",
                new XAttribute("VitaminA", "1g"),
                new XAttribute("Calcium", "2g"),
                new XAttribute("Iron", "1g")),
```

```
      new XElement("TotalFat", "16g",
         new XAttribute("SaturatedFat", "7g"),
         new XAttribute("TransFat", "9g"))
   ) );
// Add new type of Icecream to the existing XML
ClassicIcecreams.Add(
      new XElement("Icecream",
      new XElement("Name", "Banana Split Icecream"),
      new XElement("Cholesterol", "58mg"),
      new XElement("TotalCarbohydrates", "24g"),
      new XElement("Protein", "6g",
         new XAttribute("VitaminA", "2g"),
         new XAttribute("Iron", "1g")),
      new XElement("TotalFat", "13g",
         new XAttribute("SaturatedFat", "7g"),
         new XAttribute("TransFat", "6g"))
));
```

After creating the XML element, save it as an XML file under a directory using the code below:

```
// Save that as an XML file
ClassicIcecreams.Save(@"C:\ClassicIcecreamsList.xml");
```

Check if the text file we are going to create already exists in the directory. If the file does not exist, we will proceed with constructing the query and fetching rows. Then we can create a text file and write into it.

```
// Text file to store the xml content
string path = @"c:\ClassicIcecreamsList.txt";
if (!File.Exists(path))
{
    // Load the XML file into an XElement
    XElement LoadClassicIcecreamsList =
        XElement.Load(@"C:\ClassicIcecreamsList.xml");
```

Using LINQ, query the XML element to fetch the records one-by-one. On fetching the records, we have to separate the fields or values using the comma delimiter so that we can identify fields next time we read it. To convert the XML element into delimited strings, we have used the formatting of `string` object. Pass all different element values as parameters to the format method.

Note that the following code fetches even the attribute values of the XML elements, and passes that as strings to the `Format` method. The last line in the `Select` statement uses the `Environment.NewLine` method to include a line break at the end of each record. The aggregate operator is used to append all values of the child elements and then format it with a comma delimiter.

```
// Using Linq query the XElement to fetch records with the comma
    delimiter string Ice = (from el in LoadClassicIcecreamsList.
        Elements("Icecream")
            select String.Format("{0}, {1}, {2}, {3}, {4}, {5}, {6} {7}",
            (string)el.Element("Name"),
            (string)el.Element("Cholesterol"),
            (string)el.Element("TotalCarbohydrates"),
            (string)el.Element("Protein").Attribute("VitaminA"),
            (string)el.Element("Protein").Attribute("Iron"),
            (string)el.Element("TotalFat").Attribute("SaturatedFat"),
            (string)el.Element("TotalFat").Attribute("TransFat"),
            Environment.NewLine
    )
    ).Aggregate(
        new StringBuilder(),
        (sb, s) => sb.Append(s),
        sb => sb.ToString()
    );
```

Now we have all the XML element values as delimited strings. Using the StreamWriter, we can write the string into a text file.

We can also create the CSV file using the `File.WriteAllText` method by passing the string containing the text.

```
// Add all the records stored in the string Ice to the text file
    using (StreamWriter sw = File.CreateText(path))
    { sw.WriteLine(Ice); }
// Create a csv file and write all the records stored in the string Ice
File.WriteAllText(@"C:\Icecreams.csv", Ice);
}
```

After writing the string into the text file, the text file will contain the following text:

```
Chocolate Fudge Icecream, 50mg, 35g, 3g, 1g, 9g, 11g
Vanilla Icecream, 65mg, 26g, 1g, 1g, 7g, 9g
Banana Split Icecream, 58mg, 24g, 2g, 1g, 7g, 6g
```

Reading from CSV Files

We have seen how to create text and CSV files and write XML elements into it. Now we will see how to get details from the CSV file and construct an XML from it. Using the functional construction of XElement, we can easily build the XML from the CSV data source. The only thing is, we should know the field names for the values we have in the CSV file. The sample code below explains how to read from a file and construct the XML. The first thing is to load the CSV file into an array of strings. Using the query, fetch records from the strings. On fetching each record, we have to split the strings according to the comma delimiter. So the `Split` method is used for spliting the string into a field array. Then from the field array, we can take individual fields using the array index and assign them to the corresponding XML element.

```
// Read all the details from CSV to string array
string[] source = File.ReadAllLines(@"C:\Icecreams.csv");
// Using Query get all the field values and assign that to elements
XElement ice = new XElement("Icecreams",
    from str in source
    let fields = str.Split(',')
    select new XElement("Icecream",
        new XElement("Name", fields[0]),
        new XElement("Cholesterol", fields[1]),
        new XElement("TotalCarbohydrates", fields[2]),
        new XElement("Protein",
            new XAttribute("VitaminA", fields[3]),
            new XAttribute("Iron", fields[4])),
        new XElement("TotalFat",
            new XAttribute("SaturatedFat", fields[5]),
            new XAttribute("TransFat", fields[6]))
        )
    );
// Save the XML tree as xml file
ice.Save(@"c:\icecreamxml.xml");
```

Eexecuting this code will create the `icecreamxml.xml` file. The contents would be as follows:

```
<?xml version="1.0" encoding="utf-8"?>
<Icecreams>
  <Icecream>
    <Name>Chocolate Fudge Icecream</Name>
    <Cholesterol> 50mg</Cholesterol>
    <TotalCarbohydrates> 35g</TotalCarbohydrates>
    <Protein VitaminA=" 3g" Iron=" 1g" />
    <TotalFat SaturatedFat=" 9g" TransFat=" 11g " />
  </Icecream>
  <Icecream>
    <Name>Vanilla Icecream</Name>
    <Cholesterol> 65mg</Cholesterol>
    <TotalCarbohydrates> 26g</TotalCarbohydrates>
```

```
      <Protein VitaminA=" 1g" Iron=" 1g" />
      <TotalFat SaturatedFat=" 7g" TransFat=" 9g " />
   </Icecream>
   <Icecream>
      <Name>Banana Split Icecream</Name>
      <Cholesterol> 58mg</Cholesterol>
      <TotalCarbohydrates> 24g</TotalCarbohydrates>
      <Protein VitaminA=" 2g" Iron=" 1g" />
      <TotalFat SaturatedFat=" 7g" TransFat=" 6g " />
   </Icecream>
 </Icecreams>
```

LINQ to XML Events

LINQ to XML is mainly used for manipulating and navigating through XML tree. There are chances that many queries may try to access the same XML tree. In this situation, we always like to be notified about changes that happens to the XML data on which our query depends. LINQ provides the feature of associating events to the XML. There are two types of events that can be set to the XML when there is a change to the XML tree.

Events can be added to any instance of an XObject. The event handler will receive the events for modifications to that XObject and any of its descendants. The following events are raised when the XML tree is modified.

- Changing — occurs just before changing the XObject or any of its descendants.
- Changed — occurs when the XObject or any of its descendants have changed.

There are different objects and types used when we work with events. These types are used for getting the event type, information about the change, and the information about the object that's affected by the change.

- XObjectChange, provides the event type when an event is raised for an XObject.
- XObjectChangeEventArgs, provides data for the changing and changed events.
- XObjectChangeEventHandler, represents the method that will handle the events.

Following is the `ClassicIcecreams` XML element which contains information about an ice-cream type.

```
// Create a sample XML
        XElement ClassicIcecreams =
            new XElement("Icecreams",
            new XElement("Icecream",
            new XElement("Name", "Chocolate Fudge Icecream"),
            new XElement("Ingredients", "cream, milk, sugar, corn
            syrup, cellulose gum..."),
            new XElement("Cholesterol", "50mg")
        )
    );
```

For this XML tree, we will associate the changing and changed event so that we know about any change when it happens to the XML tree.

Create the new `XObjectChangeEventHandler` and associate it with the changing event of the XML element. This handler has a delegate which takes two parameters — one is of type object, and the other is of type `XObjectChangeEventArgs`. So if any change occurs to the `ClassicIcecreams` XML tree, this changing event fires just before the actual change. This event will display information like the sender's name and the operation that is making the object change. The type of the operation is taken from the `XObjetChangeEventArgs` argument.

```
// Create a Changing event for the ClassicIcecreams
element
// Show message with details that will be changing
ClassicIcecreams.Changing += new XObjectChangeEventHandler(
    delegate(object objSender, XObjectChangeEventArgs args)
    {
        XElement eleSend = (XElement)objSender;
        MessageBox.Show("XML is Changing " + " \n " +
        " Sender: " + eleSend.Name.LocalName +
        " Operation: " + args.ObjectChange.ToString(),,
            "Changing Event");
    }
);
```

Create another new `XObjectChangeEventHandler` with the similar parameters and types as we used for the previous example. This event handler is for handling the changed event of the XML tree. Assign this event to the `Changed event` property of the XML. This event will be fired after changing the XML tree. Here, also, we are displaying the sender's name and the change operation that caused the event to fire.

```
// Create a Changed event for the ClassicIcecreams element
// Show message with the details that got changed
ClassicIcecreams.Changed += new XObjectChangeEventHandler(
```

```
    delegate(object objSend, XObjectChangeEventArgs args)
    {
        XElement eleSend = (XElement)objSend;
        MessageBox.Show(" XML Changed " + "\n " +
          " Sender: " + eleSend.Name.LocalName +
          " Change: " + args.ObjectChange.ToString(), "Changed Event");
    }
);
```

Now create a new XML element which has the same number of elements and attributes. We will use this new element to raise events on the original XML element.

```
// Create a new XML element
XElement NewIcecream = new XElement("Icecream1",
        new XElement("Name", "Vanilla Icecream"),
        new XElement("Ingredients", "vanilla extract, guar gum,
          cream, nonfat milk, sugar, locust bean gum, carrageenan,
          annatto color..."),
        new XElement("Cholesterol", "65mg")
);
```

Now add the new element to the existing `ClassicIcecream` element so the event gets fired.

```
        // Add the new element to the ClassicIcecreams so that
        the events get fired
        ClassicIcecreams.Add(NewIcecream);
```

At once, when we try to add new elements to the existing `ClassicIcecream` element, the `changing event` fires just before the change happens. The raised event will show a message similar to the one below:

```
        // Remove an element from the ClassicIcecreams element so
        that the events get fired
        ClassicIcecreams.Element("Icecream").Remove();
}
```

XML Literals and Embedded Expressions in Visual Basic

Visual Basic supports XML to be added to the code by XML literals. This makes it easier to create XML elements, documents and fragments as we have the code and XML together without any additional dependency. Visual Basic compiles the XML Literals to LINQ to XML Objects. LINQ to XML provides a simple object model by which we can manipulate the XML data.

The following code shows a sample of XML literals added to the Visual Basic code which gives a LINQ to XML `XElement` object. We just have to type or copy the XML directly to the code section. An XML literal does not require a line continuation character. This helps us copy the XML into code without any changes or updates to the XML. If we add the line continuation character to the XML, the compiler will treat the line continuation character as part of the XML. In this example, we have not used any line continuation character in the XML literal.

```
Dim raisinIcecream As XElement = _
<Icecream>
    <Name>Rum Raisin Ice Cream</Name>
    <Ingredients>Rum, guar gum, milk, alomnds, sugar,
    raisins, honey, chocolate, annatto color...</Ingredients>
    <Cholesterol>49mg</Cholesterol>
    <TotalCarbohydrates>28g</TotalCarbohydrates>
    <Protein VitaminA="2g" Iron="4g">6g</Protein>
    <TotalFat SaturatedFat="5g" TransFat="3g">8g</TotalFat>
</Icecream>
```

Visual Basic also provides an additional feature of adding expressions to XML literals. This helps us to add dynamic content to the XML literal. For example, the following XML literal uses embedded expressions to crate the XML element from the parameter values passed to the method. When we add expression to the literal, we also get the IntelliSense help from Visual Studio to easily select the elements.

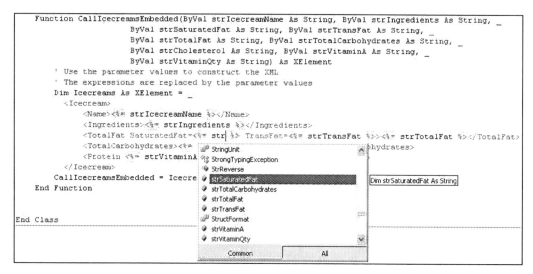

Following is the sample of an XML, created by passing the values to
`CallIcecreamsEmbedded,` which returns the `XElement`.

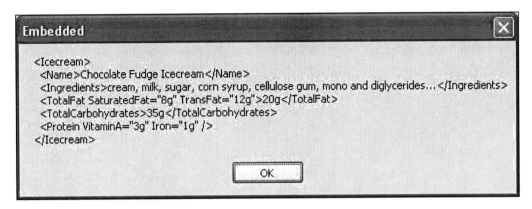

The expressions value can be a simple text, or it can be a query. The query can be
used to build the XML and the result can be an XML literal. The following code
shows a sample of an XML literal which uses the query in expressions to build XML
by fetching details from the `Icecreams` XML.

```
Dim Icecreams1 As XElement = _
<Icecreams>
    <%= From c In Icecreams.Elements("Icecream") _
        Select New XElement("Icecream", _
        c.Element("Name").Value.ToUpper()) %>
</Icecreams>
```

Summary

In this chapter, we saw information and examples on programming with LINQ to
XML. We have seen the advantages of Functional Construction in constructing the
XML tree and navigating through the XML tree. We also manipulated the XML data
in the XML tree using `XElement` and `XAttribute` object properties. We saw some
examples for querying the XML using LINQ provided query operators. We also
learned importing and exporting data from different data sources like dictionaries,
databases objects, and CSV files. Lastly we saw different events that can be fired
when modifying the XML tree. With all these features provided by LINQ to XML,
we can easily manipulate XML data through .NET code.

4
LINQ to SQL

LINQ to SQL takes care of translating LINQ expressions to equivalent T-SQL and passing it on to the database for execution and then returning the results back to the calling application by tracking changes made to the objects. LINQ to SQL reduces a lot of programming time. It comes with two different design time tools which are used for converting the relational database objects into object definitions.

LINQ to SQL, not only provides the feature of querying or referring to the relational objects, but it also has the ability to create a database and database objects. In this chapter, we'll examine some of the features that are involved in creating the entity objects, populating data to the database tables, querying and manipulating data in the database, and so on.

Working with Databases Using DataContext

DataContext is an object that corresponds to the relational database object by which all other objects are referred to or accessed. It takes a string or a connection object that implements IDbConnection as the parameter to connect to a particular database object. It takes care of translating the Language Integrated Queries into T-SQL queries to execute against the SQL Server 2000 or 2005 database, and then translating the results back to the calling application.

We can have the strongly typed DataContext, which has the definition of all objects in the database. It's not only used for accessing existing tables of the database, but is also for creating a new database. DataContext is a collection of all the objects of the database.

Following is the code example that refers to the `Icecreams` database and then points to the `Categories` table:

```
DataContext dataCon = new DataContext("Data Source=.\sqlexpress;
Initial Catalog=IceCreams; Integrated Security=true");
```

This DataContext is not strongly typed; so, if we want to refer to a table in the database, we should use the `GetTable` method of the DataContext, and then refer to a table.

```
Table<Categories> categories = dataCon.GetTable<Categories>();
```

To avoid using this method of referring to the database table, we can use strongly typed DataContext:

```
IceCreams dataBase = new IceCreams("Data Source=.\
sqlexpress;Initial Catalog=IceCreams;Integrated Security=true");
```

We can make use of the `web.config` or `app.cofig`, depending on whether the application is web-based or desktop-based, to store the connection string and referring to that for the connection string parameter. The `dataBase` data context as shown in the above code, is a strongly typed DataContext which has all the table collections declared in it. A sample of the DataContext would look like this:

```
public class IceCreams: DataContext
{
  public Table<Categories> Categories;
  public Table<Items> Items;
  public IceCreams(string connection) : base(connection) {}
}
```

The queries which use the above DataContext can directly point to the database tables without using the `GetTable` method.

The `Icecreams` DataContext contains three different table collections declared in it. All three tables should have it's definition with columns and it's attributes.

Before we go into details of other properties of DataContext, we will see what are entity classes and how we can use that to refer to the database objects.

Entity Classes

Entity classes are the objects which represent the database tables. In the previous example, the table collections of the `Icrecreams` data context, contain three tables for which we need to add the definitions of each table with its columns and its attributes.

`System.Data.Linq.Mapping` is the namespace that contains the definition for all the attributes. We have to include this in the project to specify the attributes.

The definition of the `Categories` table would look like this:

```
[Table(Name = "Categories")]
  public class Categories
  {
    private int categoryID;
    private string category;
    private string description;
    [Column(Name= "CategoryID", IsPrimaryKey=true,
     IsDbGenerated=true, DbType="int NOT NULL
     IDENTITY",CanBeNull=false)]
      public int CategoryID
      {
        get { return categoryID; }
        set { categoryID = value; }
      }
    [Column(Name="Category", DbType="nvarchar(1000)")]
      public string Category
      {
        get { return category; }
        set { category = value; }
      }
    [Column(Name="Description", DbType="nvarchar(1000)")]
      public string Description
      {
        get { return description; }
        set { description = value; }
      }
  }
```

The class should be defined with the `Table` attribute with the `Name` property. The `Name` property value corresponds to the database table name. If not specified, it is assumed that the table name is same as the class name. Once the table is defined, the fields or columns of the table should be defined similarly. To define the columns, a name should be given, and in addition to that, we should also specify the exact type of the table column which corresponds to the T-SQL column declaration. There are other properties like `IsDbGenerated` to mention the field value that is auto-generated during record insertion.

All these properties are the same as the properties, declared by the T-SQL for the database objects. Some properties like **type of the column** and `IsDbGenerated` should be specified only while creating a new database.

The instances of classes declared as tables can be stored in the database. These instances are called entities, and the classes are called entity classes.

We will define the `Items` entity as follows:

```
[Table(Name = "Items")]
  public class Items
  {
     [Column(Name = "ItemID", IsPrimaryKey = true, IsDbGenerated =
     true, DbType = "int NOT NULL IDENTITY", CanBeNull = false)]
      public int ItemID;
     [Column(Name = "CategoryID")]
       public int CategoryID;
      [Column(Name = "Name", DbType = "nvarchar(1000)")]
       public string Name;
      [Column(Name = "Ingredients", DbType = "nvarchar(1000)")]
       public string Ingredients;
      [Column(Name = "ServingSize", DbType = "nvarchar(1000)")]
       public string ServingSize;
      [Column(Name = "TotalFat", DbType = "int")]
       public int TotalFat;
      [Column(Name = "Cholesterol", DbType = "int")]
       public int Cholesterol;
      [Column(Name = "TotalCarbohydrates", DbType = "int")]
       public int TotalCarbohydrates;
      [Column(Name = "Protein", DbType = "int")]
       public int Protein;
  }
```

All tables may not have auto-generated key fields. If the table has an auto-generated field, the insert operation should not insert any value to the field which has the `IsDbGenerated` property, set to true. In this case, we can restrict assigning values to the table columns. All columns should be defined as properties of the entity class. The identity or auto-generated column should not have any definition for the set method which will avoid setting any values to the property. Following is an example for creating the same `Item` class as above, but using smart properties. Smart properties are auto-implemented properties that do not have any private fields declared specifically.

```
[Table(Name = "Items")]
  public class Items
  {
     [Column(Name = "ItemID", IsPrimaryKey = true, IsDbGenerated =
     true, DbType = "int NOT NULL IDENTITY", CanBeNull = false)]
     public int ItemID { get; private set;
  }
[Column(Name = "CategoryID")]
```

```
   public int CategoryID { get; set; }
[Column(Name = "Name", DbType = "nvarchar(1000)")]
   public string Name { get; set; }
[Column(Name = "Ingredients", DbType = "nvarchar(1000)")]
   public string Ingredients { get; set; }
[Column(Name = "ServingSize", DbType = "nvarchar(1000)")]
   public string ServingSize { get; set; }
[Column(Name = "TotalFat", DbType = "nvarchar(1000)")]
   public string TotalFat { get; set; }
[Column(Name = "Cholesterol", DbType = "nvarchar(1000)")]
   public string Cholesterol { get; set; }
[Column(Name = "TotalCarbohydrates", DbType = "nvarchar(1000)")]
   public string TotalCarbohydrates { get; set; }
[Column(Name = "Protein", DbType = "nvarchar(1000)")]
   public string Protein { get; set; }
}
```

Attributes

We have seen some attributes and their properties for creating entity classes. There are a lot of other attributes and properties that support the creation of entity classes. These attributes are used by LINQ to SQL to create corresponding SQL queries in the database that relate to the entity objects. All attributes are defined in the `System.Data.Linq.Mapping` namespace.

Database Attribute

The database attribute is an attribute that specifies the database into which we should look for the objects and data. The database can also be specified by the connection. But if it is not specified by the connection, by default the name specified by the attribute will be taken as the database. This attribute can be applied on strongly-typed DataContext. Database attribute has a `Name` property which gives the name for the database.

```
[Database(Name="Deserts")]
   public class Deserts: DataContext
   {
     public Table<Categories> Categories;
     public Table<Items> Items;
```

The `Database` attribute is optional here. `Deserts` is the name of the database. If this attribute is not specified, by default the name of the `Deserts` DataContext class will be taken as the name of the database.

It is always better to use a connection string to connect to a specific database. The above example illustrates the usage of database attribute in LINQ to SQL.

Table Attribute

This is similar to database attribute. It refers to the individual table or view in the database. It can be applied on the entity class, which can refer to the database table or view.

```
[Table(Name="Categories")]
public class Categories
  {
     [Column(Name= "CategoryID", IsPrimaryKey=true,
      IsDbGenerated=true, DbType="int NOT NULL IDENTITY",
      CanBeNull=false)]
        public int CategoryID{ get ; private set ; }
  }
```

`Categories` is the entity class on which the `Table` attribute is applied, to specify the corresponding database table objects. If the attribute is not specified, the class will be taken by default as the table.

All classes that have the table attribute defined are considered as persistent classes by LINQ to SQL. The mapping is done for a single table only. Each entity class must be mapped to only one class. We cannot have multiple classes mapping to the same table in the database.

It is always good practice to use the same name as the database table for the entity class, or leave the name of the table attribute undefined and give the same class name to the database table object.

Column Attribute

In the `Categories` entity class given previously, we have a `CategoryID` column which represents the actual column of the database table. But to specify what type of column it is and what the behaviour of the column should be, we have different properties for the column attribute.

Property	Description
Name	This property is used to specify the name of the column. This property is optional. It takes the class member name as default if the name property is not mentioned.
Storage	This property is used to specify the variable or the object in which the column value is stored. By default, all the values are set by the public property of the class member. Using this property, we can directly access the storage member and can override the access method.

Property	Description
DbType	This specifies type of the database column. It is the same as the text used to define the column using T-SQL. If not specified, the same type will be taken as the one defined by the member of the entity class. DLINQ will take care of converting it to the equivalent T-SQL type.
IsPrimaryKey	This is a boolean property that specifies whether the column is a key column for the table or not. Each table will have a primary key that is unique to identify the table rows. This property is set to true if it is a part of the primary key. If more than one member has this property set to true, it means that the members are a part of the composite primary key.
IsDbGenerated	Usually, primary key values of the tables are auto-generated. It means that the value will be generated by the system whenever there is a new row inserted to the table. This property can be applied to the database column which has the primary key property set to true.
IsVersion	This is to specify the timestamp property of the column. The column having the timestamp property shows the version of the row. On every update that happens to a row of the table, the timestamp will get updated with a new value.
updateCheck	This is to detect the conflicts by optimistic concurrency. There is a timestamp or IsVersion=true property which gives the version of the row to identify the conflict. In case none of the columns are specified as IsVersion=true, then the version has to be identified by comparing the old value with the current value of the column/member. To specify which member should be used for detecting the conflicts by LINQ to SQL, the member should be given an updateCheck value. It has three different enumerated values. • Always — always use this column for conflict detection. • Never — never use this column for conflict detection. • WhenChanged — use this column only when the value is changed by the application.
IsDiscriminator	This boolean value determines if the member holds a discriminator value for a LINQ to SQL inheritance hierarchy.
CanBeNull	This value can be set to true or false to indicate whether the column allows a null value or not.
TypeId	This is used to get the unique identifier when implemented in the derived class.
Expression	This is used to define the column which is a computed column in the database.

We have used different attributes and properties for members of the entity classes to define the database tables and the classes.

```
[Column(Name = "ItemID", IsPrimaryKey = true, IsDbGenerated = true,
DbType = "int NOT NULL IDENTITY", CanBeNull = false)]
public int ItemID { get; private set;}
```

The previous code shows the definition of the class member ItemID. It defines the ItemID as a primary key and is auto-generated. It also specifies that the member is an identity column of type integer and is an identity.

The column can also be specified as a property of the entity class. The value is stored in the private variable while the property is a public property. We can control the access of the member value by defining the storage as private. The set method definition for the property is present even though it is an auto-generated value. This is because the auto-implemented properties should define both get and set properties, shown as follows:

```
[Column(Name = "ItemID", IsPrimaryKey = true, IsDbGenerated = true,
DbType = "int NOT NULL IDENTITY", CanBeNull = false)]
public int ItemID { get; private set}
```

Association Attribute (Foreign Keys)

The association attribute refers to the relationship between tables, using foreign keys. Association property represents a single reference or collection of references to entity classes. These properties are given as follows:

Property	Description
Name	This property specifies the name of the property. This is same as the name that gets generated when we define the relationship between the tables in SQL Server Database. This name distinguishes the multiple relationships between the entity classes.
Storage	This is similar to the storage of the column attribute. It is also used to specify the name of the storage member for the property. It is used to directly interact with the value instead of going through the public property.
ThisKey	This property has a list of names of one or more members of the entity class that are a part of the relationship on this side of the entity class. If the members are not specified, the primary key members are taken as default for the relationship.
OtherKey	This property is similar to the Thiskey property but on the other side of the entity that makes up the relationship.

Property	Description
IsUnique	This is to impose a unique constraint on the foreign key to have a one-to-one relationship.
IsForeignKey	This specifies the member as a foreign key in the association relationship.

Relationships

In relational databases, tables are linked to each other by a relationship called **foreign keys**. This will bring the parent-child relationship between the tables. LINQ to SQL supports the creation of foreign keys between tables with the attribute called **association**. This association also brings the master detail relationship between the tables.

In the earlier section *Entity Classes*, we saw the concept of creating entity classes by creating Categories and Items classes. With these classes, we can create the database. We can say that each item in the Item table comes under a particular category. So here, Categories is the master for the Items detail table in the database. To represent that, we have foreign key relationships between the tables in the database. The same foreign key relationships should also be represented between these two classes. This can be done using EntitySet and EntityRef properties.

Since the relationship is one-to-many between Categories and Items table, the Categories entity class should have an EntitySet property for Items. EntitySet is a property which represents the set of entities that is of the same entity type. Here, Items is an entity set which represents the set of items that belongs to a category entity. This property should have the association attribute defined. This attribute defines the relationship between tables.

EntityRef is a property that represents the other end of a relationship. We have set the Items as EntitySet within the Categories entity class. The other side of the relationship, that is, the Items entity class, should also define its relationship with the Categories entity. EntityRef is used for giving the reference between the entity classes.

```
[Table(Name="Categories")]
public class Categories
{
   [Column(Name = "CategoryID", Id=true, AutoGen=true,
    DBType="int NOT NULL IDENTITY")]
     public int CategoryID;

     [Column(Name = "Category", DBType="nvarchar(1000)")] //,
      UpdateCheck=UpdateCheck.Always)]
       public string Category;
     [Column(Name="Description", DBType="nvarchar(1000)")] // ,
      UpdateCheck=UpdateCheck.Always)]
      public string Description;
      private EntitySet<Items> _Items;
     [Association(Storage="_Items", OtherKey="CategoryID")]
       public EntitySet<Items> Items
       {
         get { return this._Items; }
         set { this._Items.Assign(value); }
       }
     public Categories() { this._Items = new EntitySet<Items>(); }
}
[Table(Name="Items")]
  public class Items
  {
     [Column(Name = "ItemID", IsPrimaryKey = true, IsDbGenerated =
      true, DbType = "int NOT NULL IDENTITY", CanBeNull = false)]
       public int ItemID { get; private set; }
     [Column(Name = "CategoryID")]
       public int CategoryID { get; set; }
     [Column(Name = "Name", DbType = "nvarchar(1000)")]
       public string Name { get; set; }
         [Column(Name = "Ingredients", DbType = "nvarchar(1000)")]
         public string Ingredients { get; set; }
         ...
         ...
         ...
         [Association(Storage = "_Categories", ThisKey = "CategoryID")]
         public Categories Categories
         {
             get { return this._Categories.Entity; }
             set { this._Categories.Entity = value; }
         }
         public Items() { this._Categories = new
EntityRef<Categories>(); }
```

You can see the `EntitySet<Items>` private variable, which refers to the detail, entity class `Items`. The definition for the entity set has the association attribute added to it. This attribute has the property, `OtherKey`, added to it. It refers to the primary key in the database table which corresponds to this entity class, and is compared with the related entity class. There is also a property called `ThisKey` which refers to the key field in the current table. If not specified, it automatically refers to the primary key of the table.

The `Items` table, will refer back to the `Categories` table using the `EntityRef` class. The association attribute of the `Categories` property has the `ThisKey` attribute which refers to column on this entity class. The attribute also has a property called `Storage` that shows which private member holds the value of the property. If not specified, the public accessor will be used by default. This is also used by the column property.

Both the entity classes have a constructor which is defined to create the `EntitySet` object in the `Categories` class, and to initialize the `EntityRef` object in `Items` entity class.

Function Attribute

This attribute is to specify the method in the DataContext which will be translated as a call to a database stored procedure or a user defined function. This attribute has the parameter which specifies the name of the actual database stored procedure or user-defined function.

Property	Description
`IsComposable`	This is a boolean value.
	False indicates mapping to a stored procedure in the database.
	True indicates mapping to a user-defined function in the database.
`Name`	This is of type string which represents the name of the stored procedure or the user-defined function in the database.

Parameter Attribute

This attribute is used to refer to the parameters of the stored procedure or function in the database. This attribute has two properties:

1. Name — specifies the name of the parameter, stored in a procedure or a function in the database. If not specified, the parameter is assumed to have the same name as the method parameter. In the example given under the stored procedure attribute section, the method has the parameter attribute with the name as Category and the method has a parameter Category.

2. DbType — this is to specify the type of the parameter. If not specified, it will be translated according to the type specified by the method parameter.

Inheritance Mapping Attribute

This represents the inheritance hierarchy for the entity classes. Classes can inherit from another class. Inherited classes, or derived classes, take advantage of gaining all the non-private data and characteristics of the base class they are derived from. A derived class also includes its own data and characteristics. Now the derived class can be represented by its own type as well as by base class type. Following is an example for inheriting a class from a base class.

```
public class BaseClass
{
    public BaseClass() { }
}
public class DerivedClass : BaseClass
{
    public DerivedClass() { }
}
```

The entity classes used in LINQ to SQL can have the same inheritance mapping to achieve the previous inheritance facility. The InheritanceMapping attribute is used for mapping classes for inheritance hierarchy.

Now let us say we have the Items table that can contain different item types, like Cakes and Icecreams. If we want to keep the two items having different characterestics separately in the base Items table, we can have the InheritanceMapping attribute to map these classes in the inheritance hierarchy.

```
[Table(Name="dbo.Items")]
[InheritanceMapping(Code="Icecreams", Type=typeof(Icecream))]
[InheritanceMapping(Code="Cakes", Type=typeof(Cake))]
public partial class Item : INotifyPropertyChanging,
INotifyPropertyChanged
```

```
{
[Column(Storage="_CategoryName", DbType="NVarChar(50)",
IsDiscriminator=true)]
public string CategoryName
{
get{}
set{}
}
}
```

In the previous code, the `Table` attribute shows the name of the base class which is the base table. The `InheritanceMapping` attribute, maps the classes which are derived or inherited from the base `Item` class. All classes that are mapped to the inheritance hierarchy must be mapped to a single table.

There is a property called `IsDiscriminator` set to true for the column `CategoryName` in the base class `Item`. This is to denote the base class property which discriminates the inherited classes. It means that the value of the `CategoryName` field denotes which class to instantiate at runtime. There is another property called `IsDefault` which can be set to true and assigned to any of the classes. It means that whichever class has this default property set to true, will be the default class if the discriminator value does not match with any of the expected values for the derived classes.

Creating and Deleting Databases

In the above section, we have seen the usage of DataContext and the `Table` collections for the DataContext. In the previous examples, we have named the DataContext as `Deserts` with two different table collections as `Categories` and `Items`. The entity classes represent these two tables and columns through the properties, types and attributes used. Using these details, we can easily create a new database and delete the existing database with the methods supported by DataContext object. While creating the database, it is not possible to create all types of the database objects, like user defined functions and stored procedures. LINQ to SQL does not support creation of stored procedures and functions, but it can reference it and execute it. Creating these kinds of databases is useful in situations like creating the database objects while deploying the application. We can also have runtime entity classes and create the equivalent database object using LINQ to SQL. DataContext has a method called `CreateDatabase`, which will create a database at the location specified by the connection string, which is passed as a parameter to the DataContext object. For example, create the typed DataContext object that points to the local SQL server and has the table collections.

```
private void btnCreateDatabase_Click(object sender, EventArgs e)
{
  Deserts db = new Deserts("Data Source=.\sqlexpress;Initial
                            Catalog=Deserts;Integrated
                            Security=true");
  if (!db.DatabaseExists())
  {
    db.CreateDatabase();
   }
}
public class Deserts: DataContext
{
  public Table<Categories> Categories;
  public Table<Items> Items;
  public Deserts(string connection) : base(connection) {}
}
```

Define the tables the same way as the one given in the previous section. `DatabaseExists` is a method, used to check if any database with the same name already exists in the server or not. The `CreateDatabase` method takes the responsibility of creating the new database in the server specified in the connection string. `DeleteDatabase` is a method of the DataContext which deletes the existing database from the server.

```
if (db.DatabaseExists())
{
  db.DeleteDatabase();
}
```

DataContext Methods

Using DataContext, we not only can refer to the databases, but also to many of the objects within the database. There are different methods which support this feature.

Method	Description
DeleteDatabase	Deletes an existing database from the server. The database is identified by the connection string used in the DataContext.
CreateDatabase	Creates a new database in the server.
DatabaseExists	Returns true if the database already exists and if the attempt to open the database succeeds.
ExecuteCommand	This method is very useful for executing any command at the database server. It returns the number of rows affected. The signature of the ExecuteCommand looks like this: ```public int ExecuteCommand(string command, params object[] parameters);``` Parameters can be passed to ExecuteCommand in the form of parameter objets if the database object requires any parameters for execution. An exception is thrown if the number of parmeters in the parameter array is less than what is expected by the command string. If any of the parameters is null, it is converted as DBNull value
ExecuteQuery	This method is used for executing an SQL Query. It returns output as objects which match to the entity objects. Parameters can also be passed to the Query. ```public ExecuteQuery<Object>(string command, params object[] parameters);```

GetChangeSet	This returns the modified objects from the collection of objects in DataContext. This operation returns three different read-only collections such as:
	
	```public IList<object> AddedEntities { get; }```
	```public IList<object> RemovedEntities { get; }```
	```public IList<object> ModifiedEntities { get; }```
	
	The disadvantage is that the returned collections will have the following constraints:
	
	• It will not return database-generated values like timestamps, primary and foreign keys. It requires a separate command execution.
	
	• The changed object set is computed at the time of the call only.

Method	Description
GetCommand	This command provides IDbCommand with its parameters. This method is to get the command. It does not affect the DataContext state.
	Argument exception is thrown if the argument is null. It returns only the first query command and it does not return additional commands.
GetHashCode	This method is useful for hashing algorithms and data structures as hash tables. It returns an integer for the current object it is called from, but does not guarantee to be unique.
	Objects used as keys in the Hashtable object must override the GetHashCode method.
GetType	Returns the runtime type of the current instance of the object.
GetTable	This method is to refer to any of the database table. It returns the result as an object which corresponds to the entity object defined. This method is very useful for strongly typed DataContext.
Refresh	This method refreshes the state of the object with the data in the database. It refreshes the fields and properties of the object.
SubmitChanges	Any changes made using the entity objects through the DataContext object should be sent back to the database server to restore the data. This SubmitChanges method takes care of sending the modified objects to be inserted, updated, deleted, and executes the appropriate command to update back to the database.

After creating the database, the table object would look like the following:

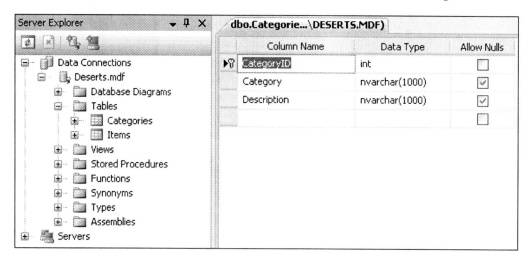

Data Manipulation

We have seen how to create the tables for storing data. LINQ to SQL supports data manipulation through entity classes. Assigning values or changing values are similar to what we do with normal classes. LINQ to SQL tracks all the changes that happen to entity class objects and sends the data back to the database. For the tables we created in the above sections, we will try to insert records one-by-one. First, we will see how to insert records to the `Categories` table. As we named the database as `Deserts`, they are of a different category such as `Icecreams`, `Cakes` and `Snacks`. The following method shows the sample code for inserting these three desert categories into the `Categories` table:

```
// Create different varieties of deserts such as Icecreams, Cakes and
snacks
private void CreateCategories()
  {
    Deserts dataBase = new Deserts("Data Source=.\sqlexpress;Initial
                                Catalog=Deserts;Integrated
                                Security=true");

// Icecreams
Categories icecreams = new Categories
{
  Category = "Icecreams",
  Description = "Icecreams Varieties"
};
dataBase.Categories.Add(icecreams);
// Cakes
Categories cakes = new Categories
{
  Category = "Cakes",
  Description = "Cakes Varieties"
};
dataBase.Categories.Add(cakes);
// Snacks
Categories snacks = new Categories
{
  Category = "Snacks",
  Description = "Snacks Varieties"
};
dataBase.Categories.Add(snacks);
dataBase.SubmitChanges();
```

the above method, `CreateCategories` first creates a DataContext `dataBase` object of type `Deserts` and points to the existing database in the server. Using the `Categories` entity class, define the categories of `Deserts` and add it to the `dataBase` data context. After adding all the categories, submit it to the database using the `SubmitChanges` method, which converts these entity objects to the equivalent SQL commands and executes at the database level.

We have created categories, and inserted records into the database. Now we have to create items for each category, which makeup the details table for the `Categories` master table. While creating the item table, we should also pass the corresponding `categoryID`, which is the auto-generate field of the `Categories` table. In order to get the `categoryID`, we have to create the `Category` entity class using the `dataBase` data context by comparing the category value. Following is an example for creating items for the category `Icecreams`:

```
private void CreateItemsforIcecreams()
  {
    Deserts dbDeserts = new Deserts("Data Source=.\sqlexpress;Initial
                                    Catalog=Deserts;Integrated
                                    Security=true");
// Query for a specific category
string category = "Icecreams";
var icecreams = dbDeserts.Categories.Single(c => c.Category ==
                                      category);
// Add Item1
Items item1 = new Items
{
  CategoryID = icecreams.CategoryID,
  Ingredients = "cream, milk, sugar, corn syrup, cocoa and chocolate
              liquor, whey, cellulose gum, mono and diglycerides,
              carrageenan, polysorbate 80,
              carob bean gum, guar gum",
  Name = "Chocolate Fudge Icecream",
  ServingSize = "4oz Scoop (113 grams)",
  Protein = "4g",
  TotalCarbohydrates = "35g",
  TotalFat = "15g",
  Cholesterol = "50mg"
};
icecreams.Items.Add(item1);
// Add Item2
Items item2 = new Items
{
  CategoryID = icecreams.CategoryID,
```

```
        Ingredients = "corn syrup, vanilla extract, guar gum, cream,
                      nonfat milk, sugar, mono & diglycerides,
                      locust bean gum, carrageenan, annatto color",
        Name = "Vanilla Icecream",
        ServingSize = "4oz Scoop (113 grams)",
        Protein = "4g",
        TotalCarbohydrates = "26g",
        TotalFat = "16g",
        Cholesterol = "65mg"
    };
    icecreams.Items.Add(item2);
    dbDeserts.SubmitChanges();
    }
```

In the above example, we have a variable called `category` initialized with the value `Icecreams`. This value is used for filtering the record from the `Categories` table. The record in which the value of the field `category` equals the value of the variable `category` will be returned to the caller and is stored in the object `icecreams`. Using this object, we can easily retrive all the column values including the `CategoryID`, which got generated during the insertion of this category record. Now using this `CategoryID` and the `Item` entity class, we can easily insert records into the `Items` table.

It is not that we will be inserting records to the tables, all the time. Many times we might need to modify the column values or delete the entire record itself. Let us see how we can update the value of a column in the `Category` table and delete an item from the `Item` table.

The following example picks the category from the `Categories` table where the value of the field `category` is equal to `Icecreams`. After picking the value of the entity object, the description of the object is modified to a new value. Similar to this, the item which has the name `Vanilla Icecream` is taken into the entity object of type `Items` and then removed from the list of items available for this category. After making the changes, all the changes are sent back to the database for updating using the `SubmitChanges` method. Refer to the following code:

```
    private void ModifyIcecreamCategoryandDeleteanItem()
    {
      Deserts dbDeserts = new Deserts("Data Source=.\sqlexpress;Initial
                                      Catalog=Deserts;Integrated
                                      Security=true ");
              // Query for a specific category
      string category = "Icecreams";
      Categories icecreams = dbDeserts.Categories.Single
      (c => c.Category == category);
```

```
icecreams.Description = "Modified Description for
Icecream Category";
foreach (Items item in icecreams.Items)
{
  if (item.Name == "Vanilla Icecream")
  icecreams.Items.Remove(item);
}
dbDeserts.SubmitChanges();
}
```

LINQ to SQL Queries

We have created the database, and database tables using entity classes and LINQ to SQL. We have also seen how to manipulate data using database table objects. Using the same database, we will see how to query the database. We have seen a lot of SQL queries in day-to-day programming for fetching records from the database objects. These queries would have been written using the SQL stored procedures, or as strings in .NET and passed as text command to the database server for execution and returning the result.

For example, fetching the items information from the database requires writing SQL statements, creating a command object and executing the SQL query through command objects. An SQL query is not LINQ query, but it is a T-SQL query. We have to depend on so many .NET objects to fetch the information from a database. The developer who writes code should also be aware of the T-SQL statements. Following is the code to fetch the item information from the database using T-SQL:

```
{
  string queryString =
  "SELECT CategoryID, Name, ItemID, Ingredients, ServingSize,
   TotalFat, Cholesterol, TotalCarbohydrates, Protein FROM Items
   WHERE (CategoryID = 1)";
  using (SqlConnection connection = new SqlConnection(
                      "Data Source=.\sqlexpress;Initial Catalog=
                      Deserts;Integrated Security=true"))
            {
                SqlCommand command = new SqlCommand(
                    queryString, connection);
                connection.Open();
                SqlDataReader reader = command.ExecuteReader();
                try
                {
                    while (reader.Read())
                    {
```

```
                        Console.WriteLine(String.Format("{0},
{1}", reader[0], reader[1]));
                    }
                }
                finally
                {
                    reader.Close();
                }
            }
        }
```

LINQ to SQL queries can be used in situations where we have to build and execute
a query from the front end application. By this, we can avoid building SQL query
strings. For example, the following code fetches records from the `Items` table were
the category is equal to `Icecreams`. This is an equivalent of the previous example for
fetching the `items`' information using T-SQL queries in .Net 1.1 and
2.0 Framework.

```
    private void SampleQueries()
    {
        Deserts db = new Deserts("Data Source=.\sqlexpress;Initial
        Catalog=Deserts;Integrated Security=true ");
        var icecreams = from ice in db.Items
        where ice.CategoryID == 1
        select ice;
        foreach (var itms in icecreams)
        {
            System.Console.Writeline(itms.Name) ;
        }
    }
```

`CategoryID` for the `icecreams` category items is passed as the parameter to the
`where` clause of the query where it will match the items and then retrieve the records.
The query is just an expression against the variable of type `Items`. Here the variable
`icecreams` is actually of type `Item`. The actual query will get executed when the
`foreach` statement is called. This is similar to the command object in ADO.NET. First
the command text will be passed as a parameter to the command object. The actual
execution of the command takes place only when any of the execution methods like
`ExecuteNonQuery` or `ExecuteScalar` is called against the command object. The
query object returns results as an `IEnumerable<Items>`.

The following figure shows the query assignment and execution:

```
var icecreams = from cat in db.Items
                where cat.CategoryID == 1
                select new { cat.Name, cat.Categories.Description };
Console.WriteLine("Items ");
foreach (var itms in icecreams)
{                          itms {Name = "Vanilla Icecream", Description = "Icecreams Varieties"}
    Console.Writel    Description  ▾ "Icecreams Varieties"
                       Name         ▾ "Vanilla Icecream"
}
```

The following figure shows a query expression assigned to the variable:

```
var icecreams = from cat in db.Items
                  icecreams {SELECT [t0].[Name], [t1].[Description] FROM [Items] AS [t0] INNER JOIN [Categories] AS [t1] ON [t1].
                  Non-Public members
Console.Writel    Results View       Expanding the Results View will enumerate the IEnumerable
foreach (var itr  [0x00000000] {Name = "Chocolate Fudge Icecream", Description = "Icecreams Varieties"}
{                 [0x00000001] {Name = "Vanilla Icecream", Description = "Icecreams Varieties"}
                  [0x00000002] {Name = "Banana Split Icecream", Description = "Icecreams Varieties"}
    Console.Writel  Description  ▾ "Icecreams Varieties"
                     Name         ▾ "Banana Split Icecream"
}
```

As it is said that the execution will take place only when the `foreach` statement executes, that is, when the actual enumeration takes place, it is also true that the execution will take place as many number of times as we have the `foreach` statement, which refers to the variable in which the query has returned the result-set which is the set, of table rows returned by the query that has been executed.

```
var icecreams = from cat in db.Items
  where cat.CategoryID == 1
  select new { cat.Name, cat.Categories.Description };
  foreach (var itms in icecreams)
    Console.WriteLine(itms.Name);
  foreach (var itms in icecreams)
    Console.WriteLine(itms.Name);
  foreach (var itms in icecreams)
Console.WriteLine(itms.Name);
```

This example displays item name values from the rows returned by the query. The query returned the result-set into the variable `icecreams`, which is of type `Items`. The three `foreach` loops use the same variable to get the items information display. Here the query gets executed three times, one each at the `foreach` statement execution. This process is time consuming, and also the execution gives poor performance. This execution is called **deferred execution**.

There is a way to eliminate this process of multiple executions for the same query. Just convert the results into an array or a list using the operators `ToList` and `ToArray`. So the previous code will look like this:

```
var icecreams = from cat in db.Items
  where cat.CategoryID == 1
  select new { cat.Name, cat.Categories.Description };
  var lst = icecreams.ToList();
  foreach (var itms in lst)
    Console.WriteLine(itms.Name);
  foreach (var itms in lst)
    Console.WriteLine(itms.Name);
  foreach (var itms in lst)
    Console.WriteLine(itms.Name);
```

Here the execution takes place only once when the resultant rows in the variable `icecreams` is converted to a list using the `ToList` operator, and assigned to the variable, `lst`. Now we can use this variable `lst` in the future, any number of times. This avoids the multiple execution of the query or **deferred execution**.

Identifying Objects

In object-oriented programming, all objects have references. So, if we assign an object to two different variables, the value is not assigned to the variables. The variables will refer to the same object using the object identity. When we execute queries, the data is returned in the form of rows from the relational database. If we execute the same query, another set of same rows is returned from the database because the rows do not have any key to identify them. The primary key which exists in the database is to identify the rows for uniqueness. So, whenever the same data is fetched from the database multiple times from the front end application, it comes as different instances. If I execute the same query three times, it will return the three result-sets with three instances.

In LINQ to SQL, we use DataContext for referring to the database objects. Here, DataContext is an object which is supposed to have object identity. Whenever a new row is fetched from the database through DataContext, it is logged in an identity table and a new object will be created. If the same row is fetched again, the DataContext will take care of sending the same instance of the object created at the first time. So the identity table is a cache table which will provide the object instances if the same object has already been created.

Queries with Multiple Entities

In the previous examples, we have seen classes with a collection of classes. For example, the `Categories` entity class has a collection of `Items` class. This kind of relationship builds the foreign key relationship at the database level. Normally in SQL queries, we have to refer to these two objects when we need a join operation for the query. As we have the collection of classes referred in the main class, we can refer to the objects easily. For example, we would be writing the query as follows to join two tables for the query without using the relationship.

```
var qry = from cat in db.Categories
join items in db.Items on cat.CategoryID equals item.CategoryID
where cat.Category == "Icecreams"
select new { itms.Name, itms.Categories.Category };
```

If we have table collections defined inside the class, the same query will look like this:

```
var query = from itms in db.Items
where itms.Categories.Category == "Icecream"
select new { itms.Name, itms.Categories.Category };
```

This query uses the table collection defined in the entity classes, and we use the object members directly in the query `where` clause. Following is the query built by LINQ to SQL for both the query expressions.

```
query = {Select [t0].[Name], [t1].[Category]
from [Items] as [t0]
inner join [Categories] as [t1] ON [t1].[CategoryID] =
[t0].[CategoryID]
where [t1].[Category] = @p0}
```

Remote Queries and Local Queries

We have seen some query expressions like this:

```
string category = "Icecreams";
Categories icecreams = dbDeserts.Categories.Single
(c => c.Category == category);
foreach (Items item in icecreams.Items.Where
(itm => itm.Protein = "4g"))
  {
    Console.WriteLine(item.Name) ;
  }
```

The first statement fetches the category details for `category` that equal to `Icecreams`. The second is the `foreach` loop, which takes care of executing the query that fetches all items falling under that category. This execution takes place at the server and then the result comes to the client application.

LINQ to SQL has a new feature called **remote queries** for `EntitySet`. In the previous example, the query would have returned the `EntitySet` of all rows from the table first, and then the filtering is applied using the `where` clause. It is not required to bring in all the records to the local application place and then to filter the records. `EntitySet` implements `IQueryable<T>`, and these queries can be executed remotely. If `EntitySet` is already loaded, the subsequent queries are executed locally. This helps us in keeping the `EntitySet` local and running the queries multiple times. Unnecessary database calls and data transfer is avoided, and also, the `EntitySet` can be serialized.

The drawback in this type of query and having the `EntitySet` local is that, data will not be the latest. This means that the local copy of data may not be the same as the one on the server. Someone might have changed the records after creation of the local `EntitySet`. The local execution is an in-memory collection which is `IEnumerable<T>`. The remote queries reflect the database changes. If the database tables are involved in concurrent changes, then different execution of the same query will result with different `EntitySets`.

Deferred Loading

LINQ to SQL supports a process called **deferred loading** which means that the data loading, or fetching the data, happens only when it is required. For example, in a query, we might have used an object which has some related objects also; but we may not be using the related objects all the time and we will be using the main object only. So the data is fetched only for the main object, but not for the related object.

Following is an example for deferred loading. The query contains the object `Categories`, which refer to the entity object `Categories` which has a related object `Items`. The query uses only the `Categories` object. The following figures show the deferred loading process in details. The query has only a `select` statement for the categories. The query expression assigned by LINQ to SQL to the variable also has only the `select` statement for the `Categories` table.

```
// Deferred Loading
var DefQuery = from cats in db.Categories
where cats.Category == "Icecreams"
select cats;
Console.WriteLine("--Deferred Loading--");
foreach (Categories categ in DefQuery)
```

```
    {
        foreach (Items itm in categ.Items)
        {
            Console.WriteLine(itm.Name);
        }
    }
}
```

In the `foreach` loop, we refer to the `Items` table which is related to the `Categories` table and also the categories entity has the entity collection for the items. When we refer to the related object `Items`, LINQ to SQL assigns the query expression as given below and then executes it query to fetch records from the table.

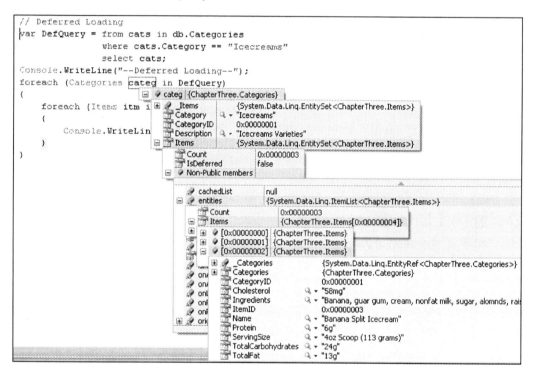

The deferred query allows us to reduce the time and cost involved in executing the queries. We can have a join between entities to fetch records, but in that case, the result would be a projection which brings a huge amount of data and not an entity result set. Entities are objects which have an identity and the results can be persisted. Projections are not entities and cannot be persisted.

Immediate Loading

It is not that we don't require related table records all the time. Sometimes we might have to fetch rows from related tables also. In certain applications, we might want to show both, master and details table records together. For example, if you want to list down the items information for a particular category you selected, you should get all the information from the table. You cannot wait for the items to get loaded after selecting the category. This kind of retrieval of data from both the tables together is called **immediate loading**. It is exactly the opposite to deferred loading. LINQ to SQL provides a LoadWith operator that allows us to load the related table's data also. The following query expression fetches the records from the Categories table, as well as the records from the related table Items that matches with categoryID.

```
using (Deserts DesertsContext = new Deserts("Persist Security
        Info=False;Initial Catalog=Deserts;Integrated
        Security=SSPI;server=(local)"))
{
   DataLoadOptions options = new DataLoadOptions();
   options.LoadWith<Categories>(c => c.Category);
   options.LoadWith<Items>(c => c.Name);
   DesertsContext.LoadOptions = options;
   Categories cat = DesertsContext.Categories.Single<Categories>
   (c => c.CategoryID == 1);
}
```

In the previous example, we used DataLoadOptions which defines the DataContext load options. It loads all the tables that have a relationship with the main table. Here, Categories entity class has an association with the Items entity. So whenever the Categories entity gets loaded, the Items entity will also get loaded for the corresponding category.

The following image shows the data loaded in the **cat** variable of type **Categories**. It clearly shows that three **Items** in the **Icecreams** category are also loaded along with the category. You can see the option **IsDeferred**, which is **false**. It shows that the loading is not deferred loading.

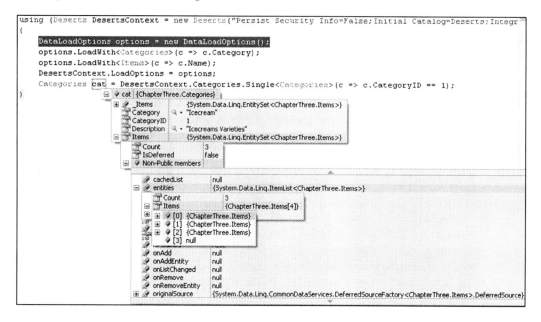

There is a disadvantage in using immediate loading or loading of any entity object with respect to performance. As there are some fields like `Category` description, `Item Ingredients` and other fields that may not be required immediately. These fields can be loaded with a delay, or maybe fetched whenever required.

This option can be set to the entities using the **Object Relational Designer** also. We will see more details about this later in this chapter, but for now, consider entities and the **Properties** page for each property in the entity. There is a property called **Delay Loaded,** which can be set to **True**, in case, delay loading is required for the entity object field, or **False** in case immediate loading is required for the field. By setting the property to **True**, the field data will be loaded with a delay.

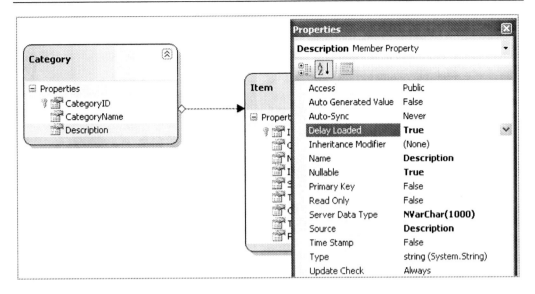

Projections

All the queries that we have seen previously are for entity objects, for fetching records from the database tables. There are situations where we may not require all columns of the tables. We might require only two or three columns out of many columns in the tables. LINQ to SQL query supports this feature for getting values of only one or more columns.

For example, we might want to know the name of the ice-creams and their ingredients. We may not be interested in any other details about the ice-creams. So, the query will look like this:

```
var projItems = from itms in db.Items
where itms.CategoryID == 1
select new {itms.Name, itms.Ingredients};
```

The equivalent query expression that is assigned to the variable would be like this:

```
var projItems = from itms in db.Items
    projItems {SELECT [t0].[Name], [t0].[Ingredients]□□FROM [Items] AS [t0]□□WHERE [t0].[CategoryID] = @p0}
            select new ( itms.Name, itms.Ingredients );
}
```

You can also construct new objects with the use of projection queries. For example, if you want to create a new object which has only the names and ingredients of ice-creams, then the query would be as follows:

```
var projectionItems = from itms in db.Items
where itms.CategoryID == 1
select new {Itemname = itms.Name, itms.Ingredients}
into newTable orderby newTable.Itemname
select newTable;
```

This query has a new object called `newTable`, which will get created based on the `Select` statement, which selects `Name` and `Ingredients` of the items. We can also order the result-set using one of the column values.

Constructing XML

We have used projections for fetching data from the database tables in different ways. Queries should be flexible enough to get the data in whichever format we like. Getting data as XML is another important requirement in applications nowadays. Using LINQ to SQL, we can easily build XML elements. The following code shows how to get data from the `Items` table into an XML file:

```
var IcecreamsasXML =
   new XElement("Icecreams",
   from itms in db.Items
   where itms.CategoryID == 1
   select new XElement("Icecream",
   new XElement("Name", itms.Name),
   new XElement("ServingSize", itms.ServingSize),
   new XElement("Protein", itms.Protein),
   new XElement("TotalCarbohydrates", itms.TotalCarbohydrates),
   new XElement("TotalFat", itms.TotalFat),
   new XElement("Cholesterol", itms.Cholesterol)
                      )
              );
IcecreamsasXML.Save(@"c:\demo\Icecreams.xml");
```

`XElement` is an object of LINQ to XML, which is the main object to create an XML file. The previous query is a mix of LINQ to XML and LINQ to SQL to fetch records and present it in XML format. The `XElement` has the direct method to save its value as XML file. The `XElement` takes care of creating the XML tree while the LINQ to SQL query takes care of fetching records for the XML tree. The final output of the above XML file will be as follows:

```
<?xml version="1.0" encoding="utf-8"?>
<Icecreams>
  <Icecream>
    <Name>Chocolate Fudge Icecream</Name>
    <ServingSize>4oz Scoop (113 grams)</ServingSize>
    <Protein>4g</Protein>
    <TotalCarbohydrates>35g</TotalCarbohydrates>
    <TotalFat>15g</TotalFat>
    <Cholesterol>50mg</Cholesterol>
  </Icecream>
  <Icecream>
    <Name>Vanilla Icecream</Name>
    <ServingSize>4oz Scoop (113 grams)</ServingSize>
    <Protein>4g</Protein>
    <TotalCarbohydrates>26g</TotalCarbohydrates>
    <TotalFat>16g</TotalFat>
    <Cholesterol>65mg</Cholesterol>
  </Icecream>
  <Icecream>
    <Name>Black Walnut Icecream</Name>
    <ServingSize>4oz Scoop (113 grams)</ServingSize>
    <Protein>6g</Protein>
    <TotalCarbohydrates>25g</TotalCarbohydrates>
    <TotalFat>19g</TotalFat>
    <Cholesterol>50mg</Cholesterol>
  </Icecream>
  <Icecream>
    <Name>Cotton Candy Icecream</Name>
    <ServingSize>4oz Scoop (113 grams)</ServingSize>
    <Protein>4g</Protein>
    <TotalCarbohydrates>32g</TotalCarbohydrates>
    <TotalFat>12g</TotalFat>
    <Cholesterol>45mg</Cholesterol>
  </Icecream>
</Icecreams>
```

Joins

When we say joins, the first thing we think about is the foreign key relationship between the database tables, which is very useful when we join the tables using queries. For example, to get all the items that belong to a particular category in the Categories table, we usually join both the tables using the query and fetch the details. However in LINQ to SQL, it is not always the case. We can join tables irrespective of their relationship. For example, we can fetch records from the `Categories` and `Items` table in which `CategoryID` is a key field in the `Category` table, and is the foreign key in the `Items` table, which identifies the corresponding items. The following code fetches the category from the `Categories` table and the corresponding item name from the `Items` table having a join on the `CategoryID` field.

```
var QryCategory =
from s in db.Categories
join c in db.Items on s.CategoryID equals c.CategoryID
select new {catgry = s.Category,itemname = c.Name};
```

The variable, `QryCategory`, in the query will contain query text which is shown as follows:

```
var QryCategory =
  from s ⊞  ● QryCategory {SELECT [t0].[Category], [t1].[Name]□□FROM [Categories] AS [t0]□□INNER JOIN [Items] AS [t1] ON [t0].[CategoryID] = [t1].[CategoryID]}
  join c ir ⊞  ● Non-Public members
  select ne ⊟  ● Results View        ⊙   Expanding the Results View will enumerate the IEnumerable
  {                    ⊞  ● [0] { catgry = "Icecreams", itemname = "Chocolate Fudge Icecream" }
        catgry ⊞  ● [1] { catgry = "Icecreams", itemname = "Vanilla Icecream" }
        itemname = c.Name          ⊞  ● [2] { catgry = "Icecreams", itemname = "Banana Split Icecream" }
  };
```

The following query is another example of a join query which extracts information from both the tables and inserts the rows into a new runtime table.

```
var QueriesCategory =
from s in db.Categories
join c in db.Items on s.CategoryID equals c.CategoryID into
categoryitems
select new { s, categoryitems };
```

The following screenshot shows a query that is generated by LINQ to SQL and is assigned to the variable **QueriesCategory**:

```
        var QueriesCategory =
⊟  ● QueriesCategory {SELECT [t0].[CategoryID], [t0].[Category], [t0].[Description], [t1].[ItemID], [t1].[CategoryID] AS [CategoryID2], [t1].[Name], [t1].[Ingredients],
  ⊞  ● Non-Public members                                                          joryID into categoryitems
  ⊟  ● Results View        ⊙   Expanding the Results View will enumerate the IEnumerable
     ⊞  ● [0] { s = {ChapterThree.Categories}, categoryitems = {System.Data.Linq.SqlClient.Implementation.ObjectMaterializer<System.Data.SqlClient.SqlDataReader>
     ⊞  ● [1] { s = {ChapterThree.Categories}, categoryitems = {System.Data.Linq.SqlClient.Implementation.ObjectMaterializer<System.Data.SqlClient.SqlDataReader>
)    ⊟  ● [2] { s = {ChapterThree.Categories}, categoryitems = {System.Data.Linq.SqlClient.Implementation.ObjectMaterializer<System.Data.SqlClient.SqlDataReader>
         ⊞  categoryitems {System.Data.Linq.SqlClient.Implementation.ObjectMaterializer<System.Data.SqlClient.SqlDataReader>.Convert<ChapterThree.Items>}
         ⊟  s              {ChapterThree.Categories}
            ⊞  _Items        {System.Data.Linq.EntitySet<ChapterThree.Items>}
               Category      ◌ ▾ "Snaks"
               CategoryID    3
               Description   ◌ ▾ "Snacks Varieties"
            ⊞  Items         {System.Data.Linq.EntitySet<ChapterThree.Items>}
```

Raw SQL Query

In some cases, we may feel that the DLINQ query is not sufficient enough to handle a query or we may just want to have a direct SQL query to be performed against the database. We used to perform this using the SQLCommand object, having the command type as text and the command text will have the raw SQL query as text. This way of executing the raw SQL, directly against the database is also possible using DataContext. DataContext has a method, ExecuteQuery, which takes the query text as a parameter, and converts the results to objects.

```
IEnumerable<Items> results = db.ExecuteQuery<Items>
(@"select c1.category as Category, c2.Name as ItemName
from category as c1, Items as c2
where c1.categoryID = c2.categoryID");
```

The output of the query will be assigned to the Items object.

Query Result

We can visually see the query text that actually gets executed at the database. LINQ to SQL takes the query expression and converts it to a database equivalent query. This tool helps us to see the query generated by LINQ to SQL for the query expression.

For example, consider the following simple query and try to execute it.

```
// Normal way of writing joins between two tables
var qry = from cat in db.Categories
join items in db.Items on cat.CategoryID equals items.CategoryID
where cat.Category == "Icecreams"
select items;
```

After assigning the query expression to the qry variable, if you place the mouse pointer over **qry**, we will get the query text, shown as follows:

The full text of the T-SQL query generated by LINQ to SQL would be this:

```
{SELECT [t1].[ItemID], [t1].[CategoryID], [t1].[Name],
[t1].[Ingredients], [t1].[ServingSize], [t1].[TotalFat],
[t1].[Cholesterol], [t1].[TotalCarbohydrates], [t1].[Protein]
FROM [Categories] AS [t0]
INNER JOIN [Items] AS [t1] ON [t0].[CategoryID] = [t1].[CategoryID]
WHERE [t0].[Category] = @p0
```

If we expand the query that is shown for the **qry** variable, we can see an option to view the results of the query. We can see the description against the **Results View** option saying **Expanding the Results view will enumerate the IEnumerable**. It means that the value assigned to **qry** will only contain the query text. It will not have the result of the query execution as long as it is enumerated.

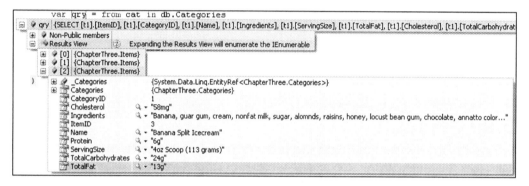

This is how the result is shown when the **Results View** is expanded.

Stored Procedures

Similar to database and database tables, LINQ to SQL also supports stored procedures. We can map the entity and DataContext classes to the database and tables which give strongly typed access to the database table objects. In the same way, LINQ to SQL also supports the feature of having methods which can be mapped to the database stored procedure. This will give a strongly typed access method and the IntelliSense feature to the stored procedures. The result-set returned by the stored procedure is also a strongly typed collection. We can create entity methods for the stored procedure manually and map it to the corresponding stored procedure or we can use the `Object Relational Designer` tool to map the stored procedures.

LINQ to SQL maps stored procedures to the methods using the function attribute, and if required, it uses the parameter attribute. The function attribute supports name property which specifies the name of the method that corresponds to the database stored procedure object.

Let us create a simple stored procedure using entity classes, created in the previous examples. This stored procedure will take Category as a parameter and return the number of items present in the database for the category. Let us name the stored procedure as GetNumberofItemsforCategory. The SQL text for the stored procedure will look like the following:

```
CREATE PROCEDURE [dbo].[GetNumberofItemsforCategory]
@Category nvarchar(50)
AS
BEGIN
declare @itemCount int
-- SET NOCOUNT ON added to prevent extra result sets from
-- interfering with SELECT statements.
SET NOCOUNT ON;

Select @itemCount = count(Items.Name) from Items, Categories
Where Items.CategoryID = Categories.CategoryID
and Category = @Category
Return @itemCount
END
```

The stored procedure takes one input parameter, @Category, which takes the category value, and returns the @itemCount that contains the number of items present in the database for the category.

The equivalent method for the above stored procedure will be as follows:

```
[Function(Name = "dbo.GetNumberofItemsforCategory")]
public int GetNumberofItemsforCategory([Parameter(DbType =
"NVarChar(50)")] string Category)
{
   IExecuteResult result = this.ExecuteMethodCall(this,
   (MethodInfo)(MethodInfo.GetCurrentMethod())), category);
   return ((int)(result.ReturnValue));
}
```

The above method has the Function attribute with the name which is same as the GetNumberofItemsforCategory database stored procedure. This method also defines the parameters with the Parameter attribute which has the property Name that has a parameter name Category assigned to it. The function uses an

ExecuteMethodCall execution method, which actually takes care of executing the stored procedure. There is a MethodInfo class that executes the stored procedure using the GetCurrentMethod method, by passing the parameter to the stored procedure. The result which is of type IExecuteResult has a property RetunValue that actually returns the value returned by the stored procedure.

The above method GetNumberofItemsforCategory, should be a part of the DataContext entity class. The DataContext class will look like the this:

```
[Database (Name = "Deserts")]
public class Deserts : DataContext
{
    public Table<Categories> Categories;
    public Table<Items> Items;
    public Deserts(string connection) : base(connection) { }

    [Function(Name = "dbo.GetNumberofItemsforCategory")]
    public int GetNumberofItemsforCategory([Parameter(DbType =
        "NVarChar(50)")] string category)
    {
        IExecuteResult result = this.ExecuteMethodCall(this,
            ((MethodInfo)(MethodInfo.GetCurrentMethod())), category);
        return ((int)(result.ReturnValue));
    }
}
```

By using the method, GetNumberofItemsforCategory inside the DataContext object, the stored procedure directly gets mapped to the method in the DataContext class.

Following is the code to access and execute the stored procedure. The method is a strongly typed method which can be accessed directly using the DataContext object, and the resultant value is returned by the method.

```
int noOfItemsforCategory;
noOfItemsforCategory = db.GetNumberofItemsforCategory("Icecream");
Console. ⊘ noOfItemsforCategory 3 ecremas: " + noOfItemsforCategory);
```

Let us create another stored procedure which will return a result-set. Here, the result-set is not pre-defined. Let's see how we can define and access the stored procedure through LINQ to SQL. The text for the stored procedure is as follows:

```
CREATE PROCEDURE [dbo].[SelectItemDetails] (@param nvarchar(50))
AS
SELECT * FROM Items where ([Name] = @param)
```

This stored procedure, returns all the rows from the `Items` table for the passed parameter value which should be the name of the item in the `Items` table.

The equivalent DataContext class method for the previous stored procedure would be as follows:

```
[Function(Name = "dbo.RuntimeShapesforResults")]
public ISingleResult<Items> RuntimeShapesforResults([Parameter(DbType
    = "NVarChar(20)")] string param)
{
    IExecuteResult result = this.ExecuteMethodCall(this,
        ((MethodInfo)(MethodInfo.GetCurrentMethod())), param);
    return ((ISingleResult<Items>)(result.ReturnValue));
}
```

The previous method used the `ISingleResult` interface, which is of type, `Items`. Using the above method, we can execute stored procedure by passing the parameter value, shown as follows:

```
// Stored procedure which returns single resultset
ISingleResult<Items> result =
        db.SelectItemDetails("Chocolate Fudge Icecream");
foreach (Items item in result)
{
        Console.WriteLine(item.Name + item.CategoryID);
}
```

`ISingleResult`, which is of the type `Items` is used here to store the result that is returned by the stored procedure. Then we can use a variable of type `Items` and loop through the returned result to get the output as we want. The following screenshot shows you this:

We will have another stored procedure that returns two result-sets. We will use the DataContext method and the entity classes to access the stored procedure result-sets. The stored procedure is like this. The stored procedure will return two result-sets; one is from the `Categories` table, and the other from the `Items` table. Following is the SQL syntax for the stored procedure:

```
CREATE PROCEDURE [dbo].[MultipleResults]
AS
select * from Categories
select * from Items
```

The corresponding DataContext method for this stored procedure would be as follows:

```
[Function(Name = "dbo.MultipleResults")]
[ResultType(typeof(Categories))]
[ResultType(typeof(Items))]
public IMultipleResults MultipleResults()
{
    IExecuteResult result = this.ExecuteMethodCall(this,
        ((MethodInfo)(MethodInfo.GetCurrentMethod())));
        return ((IMultipleResults)(result.ReturnValue));
}
```

In the previous method declaration, note the `ResultType` attribute used for the number of results expected from the output and their type. In the stored procedure, we are using two SQL queries; one for returning the categories and the other for returning the items.

To access the results after execution, we have to use the `GetResult` method of `MultipleResults`, shown as follows:

```
IMultipleResults results = db.MultipleResults();
// First Result set which is of type Categories
foreach (Categories Cats in results.GetResult<Categories>())
{
    Console.WriteLine("Cateegory:" + Cats.Category);
}
// Second result set which is of type Items
foreach (Items itms in results.GetResult<Items>())
{
    Console.WriteLine("Item Name:" + itms.Name +" Category:" +
        itms.Categories.Description);
}
```

The first `foreach` loop will refer to the first result-set of the stored procedure, and the second, will return the second result-set of the stored procedure.

```
IMultipleResults results = db.MultipleResults();
// First Result set which is of type Categories
foreach (Categories Cats in results.GetResult<Categories>())
{
    Console.WriteLine("Cateegory:" + Cats.Category);
}
// Second result set which is of type Items
foreach (Items itms in results.GetResult<I
{
    Console.WriteLine("Item Name:" + itms.I
}
```

	Cats	{ChapterThree.Categories}
⊞	Items	{System.Data.Linq.EntitySet<ChapterThree.Items>}
	Category	"Icecream"
	CategoryID	1
	Description	"Icecreams Varieties"
⊞	Items	{System.Data.Linq.EntitySet<ChapterThree.Items>}

Let us create another stored procedure which will return a result-set. Here the result-set is not pre-defined. It is based on the value passed to the input parameter. Let us see how we can define and access a stored procedure through LINQ. The text for the stored procedure is as follows:

```
CREATE PROCEDURE [dbo].[RuntimeShapesforResults] (@param nvarchar(20))
AS
IF(@param = 'Items')
SELECT * FROM Items
ELSE IF(@param ='Categories')
SELECT * FROM Categories
```

The stored procedure returns all the rows from the `Items` table if the passed parameter value is equal to `Items`, and it returns all data from the `Categories` table if the parameter value is equal to `Categories`.

The equivalent DataContext class method for the previous stored procedure would be as follows:

```
[Function(Name = "dbo.RuntimeShapesforResults")]
[ResultType(typeof(Categories))]
[ResultType(typeof(Items))]
public IMultipleResults RuntimeShapesforResults
([Parameter(DbType = "int")] System.Nullable<int> param)
{
    IExecuteResult result = this.ExecuteMethodCall(this,
    ((MethodInfo)(MethodInfo.GetCurrentMethod())), param);
    return ((IMultipleResults)(result.ReturnValue));
}
```

Following is the code for calling the stored procedure and getting the results by passing the parameter value. If we pass the value 1 to the parameter, the result would be the list of `Categories`, and if the parameter value is 2 then the result would be the list of `Items`.

```
IMultipleResults runtimeResultforItems = db.RuntimeShapesforResults(2
);
foreach (Items itm in
runtimeResultforItems.GetResult<Items>())
{
   Console.WriteLine(itm.Name);
}
IMultipleResults runtimeResultforCategories =
db.RuntimeShapesforResults(1);
foreach (Items itm in
runtimeResultforCategories.GetResult<Items>())
{
   Console.WriteLine(itm.Name);
}
```

The result view for the previous code would look like this:

User-Defined Functions

User defined functions are similar to stored procedures. We can map the method defined on a class to a user-defined function by using the function attribute. The body of the method constructs the expression and passes it to the DataContext, which executes the function expression and returns the result.

For example, following is a function that returns the `ItemName` for the passed `itemID`.

```
CREATE FUNCTION GetItemName(@itemID int)
RETURNS nvarchar(100)
AS
BEGIN
DECLARE @itemName nvarchar(100)
Select @itemName= [Name] from Items where IItemID = @itemID
RETURN @itemName
END
```

The equivalent method for the DataContext would be as follows:

```
[Function(Name = "dbo.GetItemName", IsComposable = true)]
[return: Parameter(DbType = "VarChar(100)")]
public string GetItemName([Parameter(Name = "itemID",
DbType = "int")] int @itemID)
{
   return ((string)(this.ExecuteMethodCall(this,
   ((MethodInfo)(MethodInfo.GetCurrentMethod())),
   @itemID).ReturnValue));
   }
```

If you see the attribute for the method, it is the same one used for the stored procedure. Only the name is the difference here. The execution is also similar to the stored procedure. We can call the function as follows:

```
string itemName = db.GetItemName(1);
```

Class Generator Tool

In all the previous examples, we have seen different ways of creating database objects using LINQ to SQL support. This is fine while creating a new database and its objects, and mapping the same with the entity classes. If we have a database that already exists for our application to use, we will end up creating corresponding class objects, which will consume a lot of our time. In order to avoid this, LINQ to SQL comes with a new tool called SQLMetal, which takes care of creating the entity class objects for the existing database. The same thing can also be done using the Object Relation Designer, which we are going to see later in this chapter. However the advantage of using SQLMetal is that it is a command line tool that can be used in the automated build process. All we have to do is to use the tool and provide the database name, location and format in which we want the objects. It is a command line utility that automates the task. To see the different options available with SQLMetal, type `sqlmetal /` at the command prompt.

```
 - Generate an intermediate dbml file for customization from the database.
 - Generate code and mapping attributes or mapping file from a dbml file.

Options:
  /server:<name>              Database server name.
  /database:<name>            Database catalog on server.
  /user:<name>                Login user ID (default: use Windows Authentication)
.
  /password:<password>        Login password (default: use Windows Authentication
).
  /conn:<connection string>   Database connection string. Cannot be used with /se
rver, /database, /user or /password options.
  /timeout:<seconds>          Timeout value to use when SqlMetal accesses the dat
abase (default: 0 which means infinite).

  /views                      Extract database views.
  /functions                  Extract database functions.
  /sprocs                     Extract stored procedures.

  /dbml[:file]                Output as dbml. Cannot be used with /map option.
  /code[:file]                Output as source code. Cannot be used with /dbml op
tion.
  /map[:file]                 Generate mapping file, not attributes. Cannot be us
ed with /dbml option.

  /language:<language>        Language for source code: VB or C# (default: derive
d from extension on code file name).
  /namespace:<name>           Namespace of generated code (default: no namespace)

  /context:<type>             Name of data context class (default: derived from d
atabase name).
  /entitybase:<type>          Base class of entity classes in the generated code
(default: entities have no base class).
  /pluralize                  Automatically pluralize or singularize class and me
mber names using English language rules.
  /serialization:<option>     Generate serializable classes: None or Unidirection
al (default: None).
  /provider:<type>            Provider type (default: provider is determined at r
un time).

  <input file>                May be a SqlExpress mdf file, a SqlCE sdf file, or
a dbml intermediate file.

Create code from SqlServer:
  SqlMetal /server:myserver /database:northwind /code:nwind.cs /namespace:nwind


Generate intermediate dbml file from SqlServer:
  SqlMetal /server:myserver /database:northwind /dbml:northwind.dbml /namespace:
nwind
```

SQLMetal supports two different formats for objects. One is the entity classes in different languages like Visual Basic or C# and the other is the XML format. Then functionality involved in SQLMetal is of two steps, explained as follows:

1. Extracting the information format from the database and creating a `.dbml` file. This is the intermediate file generated for customization. From this DBML file, we can generate code and mapping attributes.

2. Generating a code output file.

This advanced feature comes with some exceptions. SQLMetal cannot extract a stored procedure that calls itself. The nesting level of the database objects, like views, functions, and stored procedures, should not exceed 32.

For creating the entity classes for the `Deserts` database that we created through the previous examples, the command would look like this:

```
sqlmetal /server:.\SQLExpress /database:c:\demo\Deserts.mdf
/pluralize/namespace:Deserts /code:Deserts.cs
```

The above command will create the `Deserts.cs` file which contains the entity classes, and their relationship and definitions for the objects. This will create the classes using C# language. If you want to get the classes in VB, just rename the code as `Deserts.vb` instead of `Deserts.cs` to identify the language to be used. SQLMetal also has an option to specify the language. We can use that as well for creating the entity classes.

Using SQLMetal, we can create the DBML as follows:

```
sqlmetal /server:.\SQLExpress /database:c:\demo\Deserts.mdf /dbml:
Deserts.dbml
```

We can also use this:

```
Sqlmetal /dbml:deserts.dbml c:\demo\Deserts.mdf
```

The same entity objects created above can also be created in XML format. The command for that is as follows:

```
sqlmetal /server:.\SQLExpress /database:c:\demo\Deserts.mdf /pluralize
/namespace:Deserts /code:Deserts.xml
```

This code will produce an XML file containing all the entity objects. The output of this would look like this:

```xml
<?xml version="1.0" encoding="utf-8" ?>
<Database xmlns:xsi="http://www.w3.org/2001/XMLSchema-instance" xmlns:xsd="http://www.w3.org/2001/XMLSchema" Name="c:\demo\Deserts.mdf"
  Class="CDemoDesertsMdf">
  <Schema Name="dbo" Property="dbo" Class="Dbo">
    <Table Name="Categories" Class="Category">
      <Column Name="CategoryID" Type="System.Int32" DbType="Int NOT NULL IDENTITY" IsIdentity="true" IsAutoGen="true" IsReadOnly="false"
        Precision="10" Scale="255" />
      <Column Name="Category" Property="Content" Type="System.String" DbType="NVarChar(1000)" StringLength="1000" />
      <Column Name="Description" Type="System.String" DbType="NVarChar(1000)" StringLength="1000" />
      <Association Name="FK_Items_Categories" Property="Items" Kind="ManyToOneChild" Target="Items">
        <Column Name="CategoryID" />
      </Association>
      <PrimaryKey Name="PK_Categories">
        <Column Name="CategoryID" />
      </PrimaryKey>
      <Index Name="PK_Categories" Style="CLUSTERED" IsUnique="true">
        <Column Name="CategoryID" />
      </Index>
    </Table>
    <Table Name="Items" Class="Item">
      <Column Name="IItemID" Type="System.Int32" DbType="Int NOT NULL IDENTITY" IsIdentity="true" IsAutoGen="true" IsReadOnly="false" Precision="10"
        Scale="255" />
      <Column Name="CategoryID" Type="System.Int32" DbType="Int NOT NULL" Precision="10" Scale="255" />
      <Column Name="Name" Type="System.String" DbType="NVarChar(1000)" StringLength="1000" />
      <Column Name="Ingredients" Type="System.String" DbType="NVarChar(1000)" StringLength="1000" />
      <Column Name="ServingSize" Type="System.String" DbType="NVarChar(1000)" StringLength="1000" />
      <Column Name="TotalFat" Type="System.String" DbType="NVarChar(1000)" StringLength="1000" />
      <Column Name="Cholesterol" Type="System.String" DbType="NVarChar(1000)" StringLength="1000" />
      <Column Name="TotalCarbohydrates" Type="System.String" DbType="NVarChar(1000)" StringLength="1000" />
      <Column Name="Protein" Type="System.String" DbType="NVarChar(1000)" StringLength="1000" />
      <Association Name="FK_Items_Categories" Property="Category" Kind="ManyToOneParent" Target="Categories">
        <Column Name="CategoryID" />
      </Association>
      <PrimaryKey Name="PK_Items">
        <Column Name="IItemID" />
      </PrimaryKey>
      <Index Name="PK_Items" Style="CLUSTERED" IsUnique="true">
        <Column Name="IItemID" />
      </Index>
    </Table>
  </Schema>
</Database>
```

Either class file or XML which is generated by the tool may not have proper names for the classes which we might want to rename or modify for better understanding. This cannot be done directly while creating classes. To achieve this, we have to first generate the XML file. In the XML file we can modify or annotate it with a class and property attribute to modify the attributes of tables and columns. After doing this, we can use this modified XML file to generate the object model. This can be done using the following command:

```
SqlMetal /namespace:Deserts /code:Deserts.cs Deserts.xml
```

The SQLMetal takes all the information from the XML file and generates the class file. The XML file acts as the metadata for generating the class file. It contains attributes that can be set to change the behaviour of the tables or columns. For example, the attributes for the columns are as follows:

```
<Column
Name = "Column-Name"
Hidden = "true|false"
Access = "public|private|internal|protected"
Property = "property-name"
```

```
DBType = "database-type"
Type = "CLR-type"
Nullable = "true|false"
IsIdentity = "true|false"
IsAutoGen = "true|false"IsVersion = "true|false"
IsReadOnly = "true|false"
UpdateCheck = "Always|Never|WhenChanged" />
```

The `Table` has attributes such as:

```
<Table
Name = "Table-Name"
Hidden = "true|false"
Access = "public|internal"
Class = "element-class-name"
Property = "context-or-schema-property-name" >
```

Some of the attributes are very common to many of the elements and some are specific to some elements. For example, `Name` and `Hidden` are very common to all the elements.

Transactions

Transaction is a service in which, a series of actions either succeed or fail. If it fails, all the changes made by the transaction are undone automatically. The DataContext takes care of handing transactions. It makes use of the transaction if one is already created, otherwise it creates one transaction on its own for all the updates that happen through the DataContext.

LINQ to SQL is a new feature supported by ADO.NET. So LINQ to SQL should be able to make use of other features of ADO.NET. ADO.NET uses a connection object which takes the connection string as parameter for connecting to the database. When we create a DataContext, we can make use of the connection created by ADO.NET. LINQ to SQL will use the same connection for its queries and updates to the database. For example, the ADO.NET connection to the database `Deserts` in the local server will be as follows:

```
SqlConnection connection = new SqlConnection("PersistSecurity
Info=False;Initial Catalog=Deserts;
Integrated Security=SSPI;server=(local)");
connection.Open;
```

The `Deserts` DataContext can use the connection object for the queries and updates to the database. After performing the task, the connection should be closed by the DataContext object.

```
Deserts db = new Deserts(connection);
var icecreams =  from cat in db.Items
where cat.CategoryID == 1
select cat;
db.Connection.Close();
```

The different ways of handling transactions, are stated as follows:

1. **Explicit Local Transaction**: When `SubmitChanges` method is called, and if the transaction property is set, then the `SubmitChanges` method is executed in the same transaction context.

2. **Explicit Distributed Transaction**: LINQ to SQL queries can also be called within the scope of the transaction. The `SubmitChanages` method can be called for submitting the execution of the queries.

3. **Implicit Transaction**: When the `SubmitChanges` method is called, LINQ to SQL checks to see if the call is within the scope of a transaction or if the transaction property is set. If it is present, it executes within the transaction, otherwise it starts a local transaction and executes the commands.

Handling Concurrency Conflicts

We have seen how to save data to the database and use transaction objects to save the data safely into multiple databases. When we save the changes back to the database, it is not guaranteed that the data will remain the same, since we read it the last time. There are chances that other users might be using the same application and will be updating the same information that we are also trying to update.

Optimistic concurrency conflict occurs when we attempt to submit the changes we made, and at the same time another user has updated the same record. To resolve this, LINQ to SQL has some properties for the members by which we can easily find out the members in conflict and then handle it. To detect conflicts when the application has changed the value of the member, we have to use the property called `UpdateCheck` associated with the `ColumnAttribute` of the member. We can include the members for detecting the optimistic concurrency conflicts using this `ColumnAttribute` with `UpdateCheck` property. This `UpdateCheck` property has three enumerated values—`Always`, `Never`, and `WhenChanged`. Following are the different scenarios where we use the different properties of `UpdateCheck`.

- **UpdateCheck.Always**: Always use this member to detect conflicts.
- **UpdateCheck.Never**: Never use this member to detect conflicts.
- **UpdateCheck.WhenChanged**: Use this member for detecting conflicts only when the application has changed the value of the member.

The following code is an example that represents, the `Description` column, and it should never be used for checking the update conflicts:

```
[Column(Name="Description", DbType="nvarchar(1000)",
UpdateCheck= UpdateCheck.Never)]
public string Description
{
  get; set;
}
```

Object Relational Designer (O/R Designer)

LINQ to SQL object relational designer is the visual design surface to create the entity objects and bind the controls to the LINQ to SQL objects with relationships. O/R designer is used to create an object model in an application that maps to the database objects. Database object not only means that it can map to database tables, but we can map stored procedures and user-defined functions too. For objects like stored procedures and functions, the DataContext cannot have an entity class created, but has corresponding methods to create the expressions. The designer has its surface split into two different areas. **Entities Pane** on the left and the **Methods Pane** on the right of the surface. The **Entities Pane** , is the main pane, which displays the entity classes that adds to the DataContext. The **Methods Pane** lists the methods of the DataContext, which are mapped to the databasestored procedures and user-defined functions.

```xml
<?xml version="1.0" encoding="utf-8" ?>
<Database xmlns:xsi="http://www.w3.org/2001/XMLSchema-instance" xmlns:xsd="http://www.w3.org/2001/XMLSchema" Name="c:\demo\Deserts.mdf"
  Class="CDemoDesertsMdf">
 <Schema Name="dbo" Property="dbo" Class="Dbo">
 - <Table Name="Categories" Class="Category">
    <Column Name="CategoryID" Type="System.Int32" DbType="Int NOT NULL IDENTITY" IsIdentity="true" IsAutoGen="true" IsReadOnly="false"
      Precision="10" Scale="255" />
    <Column Name="Category" Property="Content" Type="System.String" DbType="NVarChar(1000)" StringLength="1000" />
    <Column Name="Description" Type="System.String" DbType="NVarChar(1000)" StringLength="1000" />
  - <Association Name="FK_Items_Categories" Property="Items" Kind="ManyToOneChild" Target="Items">
      <Column Name="CategoryID" />
    </Association>
  - <PrimaryKey Name="PK_Categories">
      <Column Name="CategoryID" />
    </PrimaryKey>
  - <Index Name="PK_Categories" Style="CLUSTERED" IsUnique="true">
      <Column Name="CategoryID" />
    </Index>
  </Table>
 - <Table Name="Items" Class="Item">
    <Column Name="IItemID" Type="System.Int32" DbType="Int NOT NULL IDENTITY" IsIdentity="true" IsAutoGen="true" IsReadOnly="false" Precision="10"
      Scale="255" />
    <Column Name="CategoryID" Type="System.Int32" DbType="Int NOT NULL" Precision="10" Scale="255" />
    <Column Name="Name" Type="System.String" DbType="NVarChar(1000)" StringLength="1000" />
```

Now we shall see how we can create a new application and create entity classes and methods of the DataContext.

Create a new project and add a new class `Item` of type `LINQ to SQL Classes` to the project. Now you can see the `DataClasses1` file getting added to the project. It has two files named — `DataClasses1.dbml`, and `DataClasses.cs`, associated with the project. The .dbml file is the surface for the designer which will be empty in the beginning. The `DataClasses.cs` is the file that contains the corresponding code for the entity objects and the methods added to the DataContext. Now open the **Server Explorer** and expand the database that you want to use, and locate the table and stored procedure objects. Now drag-and-drop the table objects from the list of database objects shown in the **Server Explorer** to the surface of the designer. As soon as the first object is dropped onto the surface, the DataContext is configured with the connection information using the database connection information. The entity class for the object dropped on the surface also gets added to the DataContext. In this way, we can create all entity classes for the database tables and views.

Similar to the tables and views, we can add stored procedures and functions to the surface. As soon as we drop the stored procedure or function, the designer creates the corresponding method and adds it to the DataContext. These methods are listed in the **Methods Pane**, which is on the right side of the designer. In LINQ to SQL, both stored procedures and functions are mapped to the entity classes using the function attribute. It shows all the methods added to the designer. We can hide or unhide the **Methods Pane** using the option given when you right-click on the designer surface.

Drag-and-drop of stored procedures and functions into the design surface makes a lot of difference depending on where we drop it on the surface. The return type of the generated DataContext method differs based on the place it is dropped.

1. If the stored procedure or function is dropped on the empty surface of the designer, the designer creates the DataContext method with the return type, automatically generated. This automatically generated type has the name, which is that of the stored procedure or the function with the name of the return field used by the stored procedure or function.

2. If the object is dropped on the entity class, then the designer creates the DataContext method with the return type, which is the same as that of the entity class.

We can modify the return type of the method after adding it to the DataContext. The method code generated for the DataContext would be as follows:

```
[Function(Name = "dbo.SelectItemDetails")]
public ISingleResult<Items> SelectItemDetails
([Parameter(DbType ="NVarChar(50)")] string param)
```

```
{
  IExecuteResult result = this.ExecuteMethodCall(this,
  (MethodInfo)(MethodInfo.GetCurrentMethod())), param);
  return ((ISingleResult<Items>)(result.ReturnValue));
}
[Function(Name = "dbo.MultipleResults")]
[ResultType(typeof(Categories))]
[ResultType(typeof(Items))]
public IMultipleResults MultipleResults()
{
IExecuteResult result = this.ExecuteMethodCall(this,
(MethodInfo)(MethodInfo.GetCurrentMethod())));
return ((IMultipleResults)(result.ReturnValue));
}
[Function(Name = "dbo.RuntimeShapesforResults")]
[ResultType(typeof(Categories))]
[ResultType(typeof(Items))]
public IMultipleResults RuntimeShapesforResults([Parameter(DbType =
"int")] System.Nullable<int> param)
{
IExecuteResult result = this.ExecuteMethodCall(this,
((MethodInfo)(MethodInfo.GetCurrentMethod())), param);
return ((IMultipleResults)(result.ReturnValue));
}
[Function(Name = "dbo.GetItemName", IsComposable = true)]
[return: Parameter(DbType = "VarChar(100)")]
public string GetItemName([Parameter(Name = "itemID",
DbType = "int")] int @itemID)
{
  return ((string)(this.ExecuteMethodCall(this,
  (MethodInfo)(MethodInfo.GetCurrentMethod())),
  @itemID).ReturnValue));
}
```

There are two types of methods:

1. One which just executes the stored procedure or the function and returns the result.

2. The second type is used for database operations like insert, update and delete for an entity class. This is called to store the modified records of the entities to the database.

We have seen the usage of the first option in our previous examples. Now let us try to use the second option of creating a stored procedure for insert operation of an entity class and map that to the corresponding entity class in the DataContext.

Let's create the database stored procedure for inserting records into the category table as follows:

```
CREATE PROCEDURE [dbo].[InsertintoCategory]
(   @category nvarchar (100) = NULL,
    @description nvarchar (100) = NULL
)
AS
INSERT into Categories (CategoryName, Description)
VALUES (@category, @description)
```

Now expand the server explorer and locate the stored procedure. Drag-and-drop the stored procedure on the designer surface to create the corresponding DataContext method. The generated DataContext method would look like this:

```
[Function(Name="dbo.InsertintoCategory")]
public int InsertintoCategory([Parameter(DbType="NVarChar(100)")]
string category, [Parameter(DbType="NVarChar(100)")] string
description)
{
   IExecuteResult result = this.ExecuteMethodCall(this,
   ((MethodInfo)(MethodInfo.GetCurrentMethod())), category,
   description);
   return ((int)(result.ReturnValue));
}
```

Now select the entity object and open **Properties** of the entity class. Entity class has properties like **Insert**, **Update**, and **Delete**, as shown in the following screenshot:

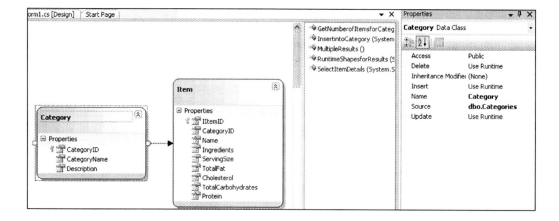

In the **Properties** window, click on the **Use Runtime** option against **Insert** property for the **Category** entity class. The **Configure Behavior** window opens for mapping the stored procedure to the entity class.

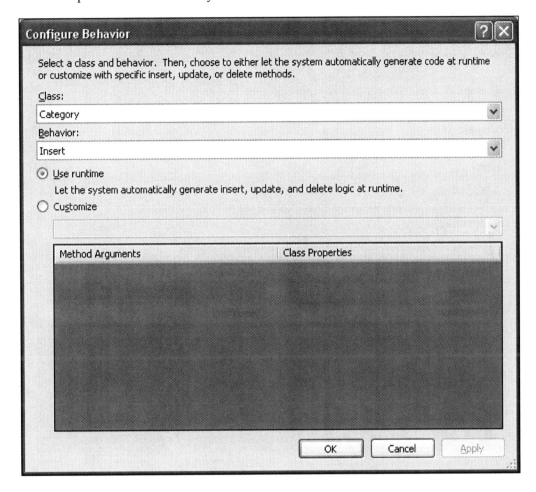

There are two options, **Use runtime** and **Customize**. If we select the **Use runtime** option, the system automatically generates the logic for **Insert**, **Update**, and **Delete** at runtime. If we select the **Customize** option, then we have to select the stored procedure from the list and configure the properties as follows:

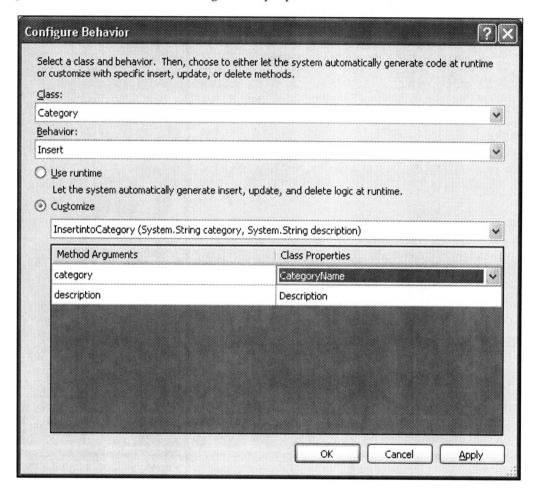

Like this, we can create stored procedures for update and delete also, and then map them to the entity class which will simplify the operation of updating the modified records of the entity to the database.

We can easily create the windows form with data bound controls using the designer. For the database and the tables created in the previous sections, we will see how we can create a windows application with entity classes and controls bounded using the **Relational Designer**. By using this designer, we can reduce a lot of our time in creating the forms with controls. We can use LINQ to SQL queries for fetching the records and filtering them. We can also bind the controls to the data source that is created using the objects built by the designer.

Choose the menu option **Data**, and then **Add New Data Sources**. From the selected data sources select the **Object** option and click on the **Next** button.

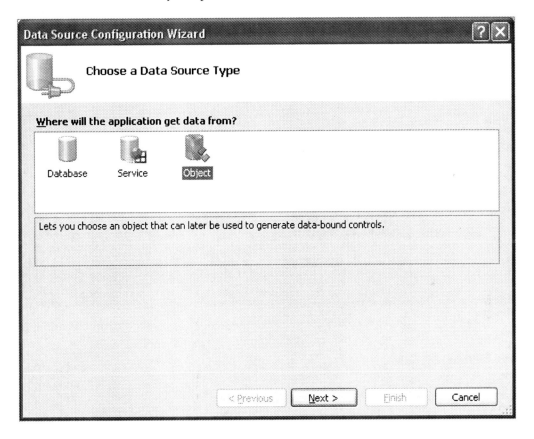

In the next window, select the **Category** entity table to add the corresponding data source and then click on the **Finish** button, so that the data source gets added to the project.

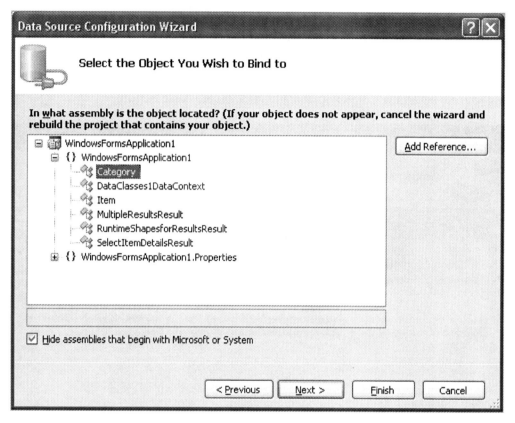

You can add as many entities to the project as you need in the application. Now open the windows form and open the available **Data Sources** list in the project using the **Data Sources** explorer.

Now open **Form1.cs [Design]**. Select the **Data** menu option, then **Show Data Sources** which will open the **Data Sources** explorer and display the **Category** data source that we created. You can see a drop-down next to the **Category** data source name which gives two options—**Details** and **DataGridView**. Let us choose the **Details** view option and then drag-and-drop the fields we need to place on the form.

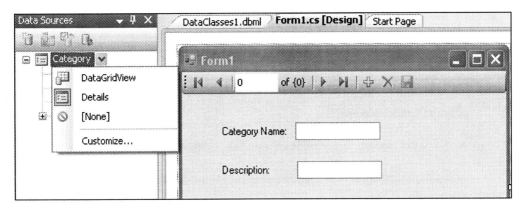

We do have display options for each field as shown in the following screenshot. Before placing the field onto the form, we can choose the control type.

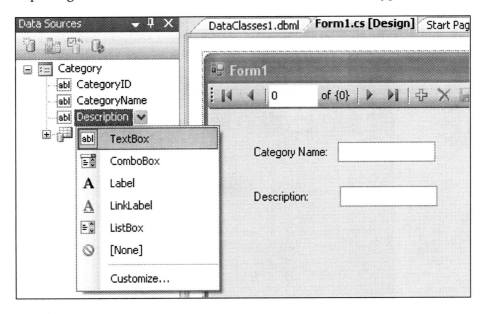

On placing the fields on the surface, we can also see a navigation bar and the editing controls getting added to the form. This automatic placement of editing controls reduces our design time for designing the form.

We have created the data source object and placed all the controls on the form. Now we need to get the data from the database through the data source and bind it to the controls. The important thing required for this is the connection to the database. We know that we have the connection DataContext which has the connection information. Add the following code to the form:

```
public partial class Form1 : Form
{
    private DataClasses1DataContext connection = new
    DataClasses1DataContext();
    public Form1()
    {
        InitializeComponent();
    }
    private void Form1_Load(object sender, EventArgs e)
    {
        categoryBindingSource.DataSource = connection.Categories;
    }
}
```

We are assigning the same connection created by the DataContext to the data source and setting the `Categories` object as the source of data. Now save the application and execute it. We can see a form with controls, with editing facility attached to it. The save option is disabled as we have not enabled it and we have not added any code for saving.

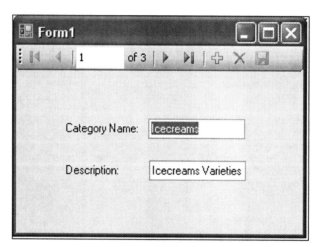

Before we look at the editing features, we will add another data source with detailed view for the items in each category that we select in the form. Now stop the execution and open the design surface of the designer.

Add the data source for the second object **Items**, similar to the one we created for the `Category` entity object. Now open the **Data Sources** explorer. We can see the **Items** data source added to the `Category` data source as it is the related detail table for the categories. There is a separate **Item** data source added for the entity **Item**.

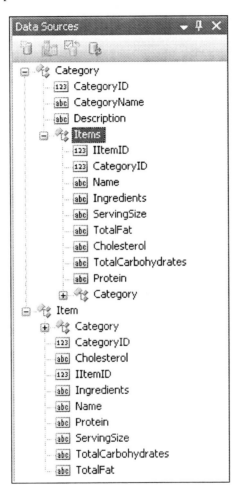

Open the form design surface using the **Data Sources** explorer, and select the **DataGridView** option for the **Item** details entity within the **Category** data source. Drag-and-drop the **Item** data source on the form, which will create the **DataGridView** to display the items which are linked to the category selected.

Now save the application and execute it. You can see the form working with the navigation feature. On selecting the category, you can see the related items displayed in the items data grid.

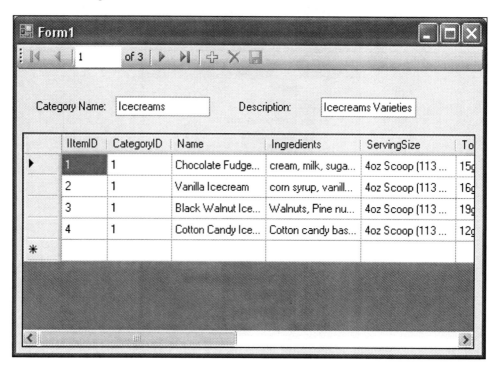

Now we have one more thing left. The **Save** button is still disabled.

Click on the **Save** button in the navigation bar and enable it. Then select the **Onclick** event and write the following code:

```
connection.SubmitChanges();
```

Now execute the application and navigate through the records. Edit the records and try saving it using the save option. We have other options such as insert and delete which we can enable by adding additional code to it. This is the simplest way of creating the application using the relational designer.

We have seen how we can create the classes and their relationship using the database objects and the object relation designer. Now we will see how we can create inheritance mapping using the relation designer. For the sake of inheritance mapping, let us add a new column to the Items table called CategoryType, which will hold the different types of items and act as the discriminator for the derived classes. Now let us see how we can drive two classes such as Cake and Icecream from the **Items** class using the object relation designer.

Open the designer surface and add two new classes to it by choosing the option to add classes as shown below:

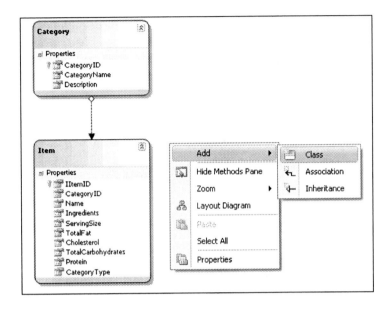

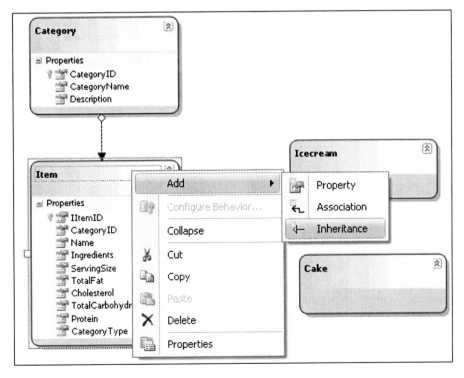

Adding the classes will not add any tables to the database, or there is no table that exists with the same name in the database. These are new entities which are empty and which are going to be derived from the entity class, Item. Now select the **Item** class and right-click to choose the option **Inheritance**. Once you choose the **Inheritance** option, you can find the dialog to select the base class and the new derived class as shown as follows. Select **Item** as base class and **Icecream** as derived class. Select the **Item** class again, and choose the option **Inheritance,** then select **Item** as base class and **Cake** as the derived class.

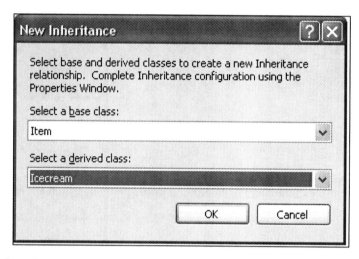

You can see the Inheritance association link between the base class and derived classes and also the derived classes are empty without any properties or methods. These classes will make use of the members of the base class.

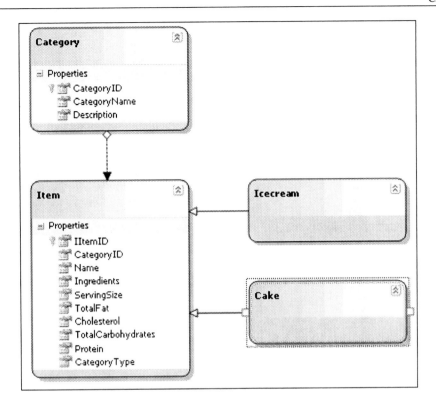

Now select the **Inheritance** arrow of one of the derived class, right-click and select the properties. In the **Properties** window, you can see different properties like **Derived Class Code**, **Discriminator Property**, and `Inheritance Default`.

Select the Discriminator field CategoryType, which we added to the entity class Item. The corresponding database column value of this field is used for discriminating the derived entity classes. The Derived Class Code property denotes the descriminator field value used to specify the derived class type. Inheritance Default is the property used to denote the default class if the value does not match the discriminator values.

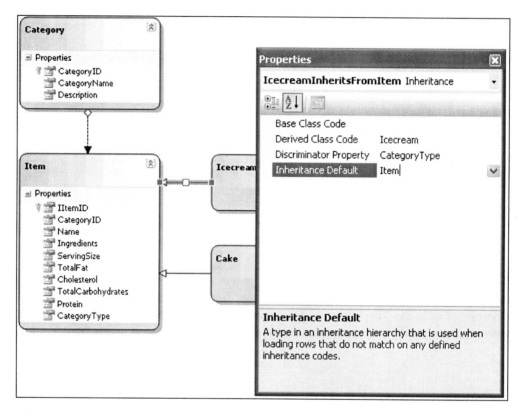

Follow the same thing to set the properties for the second derived class **Cake**. Save the file and build the project once.

To cross-check the code that is created by the object relational designer, open the class file of the designer. Following is the code for the Item entity.

```
[Table(Name="dbo.Items")]
[InheritanceMapping(Code="Icecream", Type=typeof(Icecream))]
[InheritanceMapping(Code="Cake", Type=typeof(Cake))]
public partial class Item : INotifyPropertyChanging,
INotifyPropertyChanged
{
// the members definition goes here
}
```

The code generated for the derived classes would look like this:

```
public partial class Icecream : Item
{
  #region Extensibility Method Definitions
  partial void OnLoaded();
  partial void OnValidate();
  partial void OnCreated();
  #endregion
  public Icecream()
  {
    OnCreated();
  }
}
public partial class Cake : Item
{
  #region Extensibility Method Definitions
  partial void OnLoaded();
  partial void OnValidate();
  partial void OnCreated();
  #endregion
  public Cake()
  {
    OnCreated();
  }
}
```

The derived class does not have any specific members in it. It shares the same members defined by the base class Item. We can override the members, or include the class-specific members to the derived class. By doing this, we can achieve the Inheritance feature on the entities level.

Summary

In this chapter, we have seen different features of LINQ to SQL. We have seen how to create and manipulate the database objects using the DataContext object of LINQ to SQL. We have also seen the different members of the data context and how we can make use of the DataContext members to work with database data. Also, we covered the different query features, working with stored procedures, working with user-defined functions and handling concurrency conflicts using LINQ to SQL. There are some good class generator tools like SQLMetal and object relation designer which support and provide easy ways of creating, manipulating, and working with entity objects. We have also seen some examples of creating derived classes from the base class using the inheritance mapping attribute, and also through object relation designer. Whatever we covered so far in this chapter is to give you an understanding of how we can make use of the LINQ to SQL feature for some of our database-related operations through applications. There are a lot of other features supported by LINQ to SQL, like constructing XML, lots of other queries, and handling transactions during database updates.

5

LINQ over DataSet

ADO.NET provides components to access and manipulate data from the database. These components are as follows:

- .NET framework data providers
- DataSet

There are different components in ADO.NET which provide facility to fetch and manipulate data from different data sources as per the need of the application. Connection object provides a connection to the data source, Command object gives the flexibility of executing SQL commands and other database objects, like stored procedures and user defined functions. DataReader provides a stream of data from the data source, DataAdapter acts as a bridge between the data source and DataSet. DataAdapter takes care of retrieving data from the source as well as sending data back to the source after data manipulation through DataSet. It uses Command object for executing SQL commands.

The ADO.NET DataSet provides a disconnected data source environment for the applications. It can be used with multiple data sources. DataSet has the flexibility to handle data locally in cache memory where the application resides. The application can continue working with DataSet as it is disconnected from the source and not dependent on the availability of a data source. DataSet maintains information about the changes made to data so that updates can be tracked and sent back to the database as soon as the data source is available or reconnected.

DataSet is a collection of DataTable objects, which contains rows and columns similar to the database tables. DataSet also holds primary key and foreign keys. DataSets can be typed or un-typed. Typed DataSets derive the schema for table and column structure, and are easier to program. Even though a DataSet has lots of capabilities, they are fairly limited. It provides methods for selecting, sorting and filtering data, and provides methods like GetChildRows and GetParentRows for navigation. However, for complex data manipulation, a developer has to write custom queries in the form of T-SQL and then execute it, which adds additional maintenance. Queries are represented in the form of string-based expressions which do not provide compile time checking for validity of expressions.

.NET 3.0 has support for LINQ over DataSet. There are many operators that LINQ provides for querying and manipulating data in DataSets. DataSet exposes `DataTable` as enumerations of `DataRow` objects. The LINQ query operators execute queries on the enumeration of `DataRow` objects. All these are contained in the namespace, `System.Data.Extensions`.

Before we use the LINQ to DataSet queries against DataSet, it should be populated with data. This can be done using `DataAdapter` class or other features supported by LINQ to SQL. After loading the data into `DataSet`, LINQ queries can be run on the data in `DataSet`. LINQ queries can be performed on a single table or multiple tables using `join` and `GroupJoin` query operators. In addition to standard query operators, LINQ to DataSet adds several DataSet-specific extensions to query `DataSet` objects.

Loading Data into DataSets

Before we go into the details of querying `DataSets` and `DataTables`, we have to fill the `DataSet` with some data. One of the basic ways of filling data in `DataSet` in ADO.NET is by using `DataAdapter`. Following is the code for loading data from the `Categories` and `Items` tables in the `Deserts` database, which we have already created:

```
//SQL Connection
SqlConnection conn = new SqlConnection
("Data Source=(local);Database=Deserts;Integrated Security=SSPI;");
//create Data Adapters
SqlDataAdapter categoriesAdapter = new SqlDataAdapter();
SqlDataAdapter itemsAdapter = new SqlDataAdapter();
// Create Command objects
SqlCommand categoriesCommand = new SqlCommand("Select * from
                                        Categories", conn);
categoriesCommand.CommandType = CommandType.Text;
SqlCommand itemsCommand = new SqlCommand("Select * from
                                    Items", conn);
itemsCommand.CommandType = CommandType.Text;
//Table mappings for Adapter
categoriesAdapter.TableMappings.Add("tableCategories", "Categories");
itemsAdapter.TableMappings.Add("tableItems", "Items");
// Set the DataAdapter's SelectCommand.
categoriesAdapter.SelectCommand = categoriesCommand;
```

```
itemsAdapter.SelectCommand = itemsCommand;
// Fill the DataSet.
categoriesAdapter.Fill(dataSetDeserts, "tableCategories");
itemsAdapter.Fill(dataSetDeserts, "tableItems");
```

The loading of data into `DataSets` can also be done using LINQ queries. For example, following is the code which loads the data from the `Categories` table into `DataSet`'s `DataTable`. First, let us define `Connection`, `DataTable`, and entity classes to hold `DataRows`, and define the entity structure. Entity classes are not shown here as it is similar to the one discussed in *LINQ to SQL* Chapter.

```
Deserts db = new Deserts(@"C:\demo\LINQToDataSets\Deserts.mdf");
DataSet dataSet = new DataSet();
DataTable dt = new DataTable();
DataColumn dc1 = new DataColumn();
dc1.DataType = System.Type.GetType("System.Int32");
dc1.Caption = "CategoryID";
dt.Columns.Add(dc1);
DataColumn dc2 = new DataColumn();
dc2.DataType = System.Type.GetType("System.String");
dc2.Caption = "CategoryName";
dt.Columns.Add(dc2);
DataColumn dc3 = new DataColumn();
dc3.DataType = System.Type.GetType("System.String");
dc3.Caption = "Description";
dt.Columns.Add(dc3);
```

Now write the LINQ query to fetch information from `Categories` using the `Categories` entity class.

```
var query = (from c in db.Categories
select new { c.CategoryID, c.CategoryName, c.Description});
```

Now execute the query and loop through the result and add the `DataRows` to the `DataTable` we defined earlier.

```
foreach (var result in query)
{
  dt.Rows.Add(new object[] { result.CategoryID, result.CategoryName,
                            result.Description });
}
dataSet.Tables.Add(dt);
int count = dataSet.Tables[0].Rows.Count;
Console.WriteLine(" Number of Categories :" + count);
```

DataSet comes with a visualizer, to visualize the tables in DataSet, and DataRows within DataTables. For example, following is the visualization of DataRows in DataTables of DataSet, loaded using DataAdapter.

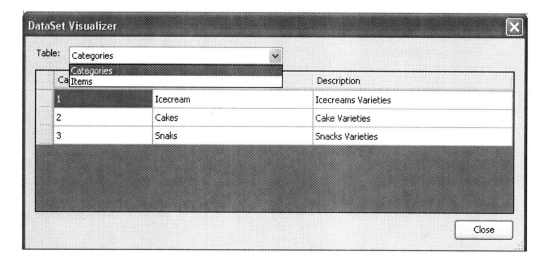

```
// Fill the DataSet.
categoriesAdapter.Fill(dataSetDeserts, "tableCategories");
itemsAdapter.Fill(dataSetDeserts, "tableItems");

var categories = dataSetDeserts.Tables[0].AsEnumerable();
var items = dataSetDeserts.Tables[1].AsEnumerable();
```

You can see DataTables listed in the **DataSet Visualizer**. On selecting DataTable, DataRows are listed in the grid that is shown in the visualizer. This is another way of verifying DataSet content.

Querying Datasets

LINQ provides many query operators and custom operators with which we can query DataSets. When we say querying DataSets, we actually mean querying DataTables inside DataSets. We cannot directly query DataTables, as it returns DataRow objects. To be a part of LINQ queries, DataTables should be enumerable and the source for the LINQ query should be IEnumerable<T>. Querying can be done on enumeration of DataRow objects so that we will have all DataColumns available for the query expressions.

```
var categories = dataSetDeserts.Tables[0].AsEnumerable();
var items = dataSetDeserts.Tables[1].AsEnumerable();
var rowCategories = from p in categories
where p.Field<int>("CategoryID") == 1
select p;
foreach (var cat in rowCategories)
{
   Console.WriteLine(cat[0] + "   " + cat[1] + "   " + cat[2]);
}
```

In the above example, `dataSetDeserts` has two tables which have details of different categories and items for each category. To query these details, we need to get the enumeration of data rows from these tables. LINQ queries work on sources which are `IEnumerable<>`. The new ADO.NET provides a feature for getting the rows enumerated by applying `AsEnumerable()` on `DataTables`. Then we can write queries based on enumeration of DataRows. The query then uses the enumerable `DataRow` object categories and retrieves the records for the category, which has `CategoryID` equal to 1. Using `Categories`, the value of the each field is fetched and displayed in the list box. `Field<>` method, which avoids casting is used here to access `CategoryID` field. We can also use the column accessor to fetch column values from the data row, but it requires casting of the columns to return values. The `Field` accessor is a generic method, which avoids casting, and supports null able types.

Following is another example of a query which involves two data tables with a `join`:

```
var rowItemCategories = from cats in categories
join item in items
on cats.Field<int>("CategoryID") equals
item.Field<int>("CategoryID")
where cats.Field<int>("CategoryID") == 1
select new
{
   itemID = item.Field<int>("IItemID"),
   category = cats.Field<string>("CategoryName"),
   itmName = item.Field<string>("Name")
};
foreach (var itmcat in rowItemCategories)
{
   Console.WriteLine("ItemID:" + itmcat.itemID + "   Category:" +
   itmcat.category + "   Name:" + itmcat.itmName);
}
```

The `join` operator used in the previous query, to fetch details from two different tables by relating a column in each table, can be avoided by introducing a relation between the tables in `DataSet` itself. This is shown in the following code:

```
// Data Relation
DataRelation CatItem = new DataRelation("CategoryItems",
dataSetDeserts.Tables[0].Columns["CategoryID"], dataSetDeserts.
Tables[1].Columns["CategoryID"], true);
dataSetDeserts.Relations.Add(CatItem);
//Now try to fetch the records as below
foreach (var cat in rowCategories)
{
  foreach (var item in cat.GetChildRows("CategoryItems"))
  {
    Console.WriteLine("ItemID:" + item["IItemID"] + "  Category:" +
                      cat["CategoryName"] +"  Name:" + item["Name"]);
  }
}
```

The `rowCategories` is the same query used in the earlier single table query methods. The first `foreach` loop is to loop through each category in the `Categories` table. The second loop refers to the `Detail` table which is related to the main table used in the query and fetches the `Detail` table records also. This can be obtained by executing the `GetChildrows` method on the main query. Then, we can refer to any of the columns in the main query as well as the corresponding records in the `Detail` table. The `GetChildRows` method uses the name of the foreign key relation created between the tables. The `CategoryItems` is the name that corresponds to the relation between the `Categories` and `Items` tables.

Sequence Operator

We can also use sequence operator to replace the above queries. For example, we can have the following query, which produces the sequence for categories:

```
// Sequence
var categoriesDetails = categories.Select(n => new
  {
    CategoryID = n.Field<int>("CategoryID"),
    Category = n.Field<string>("CategoryName"),
    Description = n.Field<string>("Description")
  });
foreach (var categoryDetails in categoriesDetails)
{
Console.WriteLine("CategoryID:" + categoryDetails.CategoryID + "
Category:" + categoryDetails.Category + " Description:" +
categoryDetails.Description);
}
```

We can also apply the sequence on joins between tables. For example, following is an equivalent query for the `join` query we saw earlier.

```
// Sequence on Joins
var rowItmCategories = categories.Where(cat => cat.
Field<int>("CategoryID") == 1)
.SelectMany(cat => cat.GetChildRows("CategoryItems"))
.Select(itms =>new
                {
                    itemID = itms.Field<int>("IItemID"),
                    categoryType = itms.Field<string>("CategoryType"),
                    itmName = itms.Field<string>("Name")
                }));
foreach (var rowItemcats in rowItmCategories)
{
   Console.WriteLine("itemID:" + rowItemcats.itemID + "  Category
   Type:" +
   rowItemcats.categoryType + " ItemName:" + rowItemcats.itmName);
}
```

Querying Typed DataSets

The structure of `DataSets` is similar to that of a relational database; it exposes a hierarchical object model of tables, rows, columns, constraints, and relationships. Typed `DataSets` derive the schema, which is the structure of the tables and columns, and are easier to program. An un-typed `DataSet` has no corresponding schema. Un-typed `DataSets` also contain tables, rows, and columns, but they are exposed as collections. Typed `DataSet` class has an object model in which its properties take on the actual names of the tables and columns. If we are working with typed `DataSets`, we can refer to a column directly as follows:

```
var categoryID = dataSetDeserts.Tables[0].CategoryID;
```

The following query uses un-typed `DataSets`:

```
var itemCategories = from cats in categories
join item in items
on cats.Field<int>("CategoryID") equals
item.Field<int>("CategoryID")
where cats.Field<int>("CategoryID") == 1
select new
{
   itemID = item.Field<int>("IItemID"),
   category = cats.Field<string>("CategoryName"),
   itmName = item.Field<string>("Name")
```

```
  };
  foreach (var itmcat in itemCategories)
  {
    Console.WriteLine("ItemID:" + itmcat.itemID + "  Category:" +
    itmcat.category + "  Name:" + itmcat.itmName);
  }
```

If it is a typed `DataSet`, the previous query is written as follows:

```
var rowItemCategories = from cats in categories
join item in items
on cats.CategoryID equals
item.CategoryID
where cats.CategoryID == 1
select new
{
  itemID = item.IItemID,
  category = cats.CategoryName,
  itmName = item.Name
};
foreach (var itmcat in rowItemCategories)
{
  Console.WriteLine("ItemID:" + itmcat.itemID + "  Category:"
          + itmcat.category + "  Name:" + itmcat.itmName);
}
```

With this query, we can avoid referencing the column using a field and casting it to the type of the database column. We can directly refer to a column in the table using the database column name.

DataSet Query Operators

LINQ to DataSet adds several DataSet-specific operators to the standard query operators available in `System.core.dll`. This is to make `DataSet` query capabilities easier. Once `DataSets` are loaded with data, we can begin querying them just as we do against the database tables using database queries. It is just another source of data for LINQ, similar to an XML data source. We can query a single table or multiple tables in a `DataSet` using `join` and `groupby` operators. If the schema of `DataSet` is known at the application design time, we can use typed `DataSet` for the queries which will be easier and will be more readable.

Some of the `DataSet` query operators used, are explained in the following sections.

CopyToDataTable

This operator is used for creating a new DataTable from the query. The properties are taken as DataColumns, and the field values are iterated and converted as data values for the columns. Following is the query which refers to `dataSetDeserts` in the `Items` table in the `DataSet`. `CopyToDataTable` operator is applied on the query to convert it to a `DataTable`.

```
var items = dataSetDeserts.Tables[1].AsEnumerable();
var query = from item in items
select item;
DataTable results = query.CopyToDataTable();
```

LoadDataRow

This operator adds `DataRows` to the existing `DataTable`. The following query iterates through the `Categories` table and adds rows one-by-one to a new `DataTable` which has `DataColumns` of the same type. This operator takes two parameters. The first one is an object that is a collection of `DataColumns`, and the second parameter is boolean for accepting the changes.

```
//LoadDataRow
var itemrows = dataSetDeserts.Tables[1].AsEnumerable();
var rowItems = from p in itemrows
where p.Field<int>("CategoryID") == 1
select new Items { IItemID = p.Field<int>("IItemID"), Name =
   p.Field<string>("Name"), Ingredients = p.Field<string>("Ingredients
") };
DataTable dt = new DataTable("TestTable");
dt.Columns.Add(new DataColumn("IItemID", typeof(int)));
dt.Columns.Add(new DataColumn("Name", typeof(string)));
dt.Columns.Add(new DataColumn("Ingredients", typeof(string)));
foreach (var row in rowItems)
{
  dt.LoadDataRow(new object[] { row.IItemID, row.Name,
    row.Ingredients }, true);
}
```

Intersect

The `Intersect` operator produces an intersection of sequence of two different sets of DataRows. It returns enumerable DataRows. Following is an example of the `Intersect` operator. The first DataTable, `tblcategoriesIntersect`, intersects with the second table, `tblcategoriesMain`, and returns the common DataRows of the two DataTables. The first DataTable, `dtIntersect`, takes the enumerable data rows of `Categories` from the `dataSetDeserts` DataSet, which we created at the beginning of this chapter. The `Intersect` operator takes the distinct enumerable DataRows from the source DataTable and then iterates through the second set of DataRows and compares them one-by-one. The comparison is done on the number of DataColumns and their types. The second parameter is the compare option for intersecting DataRows.

```
// To retrive rows which are common in both the tables
DataTable dtIntersect = new DataTable("TestTable");
dtIntersect.Columns.Add(new DataColumn("CategoryID", typeof(int)));
dtIntersect.Columns.Add(new DataColumn("CategoryName",
typeof(string)));
dtIntersect.Columns.Add(new DataColumn("Description",
typeof(string)));
var drIntersect = new { CategoryID = 1, CategoryName = "Icecream",
Description = "Icecreams Varieties" };
dtIntersect.Rows.Add(new object[] { drIntersect.CategoryID,
drIntersect.CategoryName, drIntersect.Description });
var tblcategoriesIntersect = dataSetDeserts.Tables[0].AsEnumerable();
var tblcategoriesMain =
tblcategoriesIntersect.Intersect(dtIntersect.AsEnumerable(),
DataRowComparer.Default);
foreach (var rows in tblcategoriesMain)
{
   Console.WriteLine("CategoryID:" + rows[0] + "    ItemCategory:" +
                 rows[1] + "   Description:" + rows[2]);
}
```

Union

The `Union` operator returns the union of two different sequences of `DataRows`. The operator first yields the first sequence of `DataRows` and then the second sequence. It will yield the elements that are common to both only once. Following is an example of the `Union` operator; `dtUnion` is a new table with three columns, which is the same type as in the `Categories` table, retrieved from the `dataSetDeserts` DataSet we built at the beginning of this chapter. The `dtUnion` table has one `DataRow` added to it. The `Union` operator is applied on the `categories1` DataTable with the new table created. The resultant table, `categoriesUnion`, is the union of both these tables.

```
DataTable dtUnion = new DataTable("TestTable");
dtUnion.Columns.Add(new DataColumn("CategoryID", typeof(int)));
dtUnion.Columns.Add(new DataColumn("CategoryName", typeof(string)));
dtUnion.Columns.Add(new DataColumn("Description", typeof(string)));
var catsNew = new { CategoryID = 5, Category = "NewCategory",
Description = "NewDesertType" };
dtUnion.Rows.Add(new object[] { catsNew.CategoryID, catsNew.Category,
catsNew.Description });
var categories1 = dataSetDeserts.Tables[0].AsEnumerable();
var categoriesUnion = categories1.Union(dtUnion.AsEnumerable(),
DataRowComparer.Default);
foreach (var row in categoriesUnion)
{
   Console.WriteLine("CategoryID:" + row[0] + "      ItemCategory:" +
row[1]
+ "   Description:" + row[2]);
}
```

Except

The `Except` operator produces non-common `DataRows` from two different sets of sequences of `DataRows`. It is the exact opposite of the `Intersect` operator. This operator first takes distinct rows from the first sequence, then enumerates over `DataRows` of the second sequence and compares with the first result. It eliminates the rows that are common to both the sequences. The following code is an example of the `Except` operator.

```
var tblcategoriesMainExcept = tblcategoriesIntersect.
Except(dtIntersect.AsEnumerable(), DataRowComparer.Default);
foreach (var rows in tblcategoriesMainExcept)
{
   Console.Writeline("CategoryID:" + rows[0] + "      ItemCategory:" +
                  rows[1] + "   Description:" + rows[2]);
}
```

Field<T>

When we query data for comparison, there could be a chance that the value is null. If we do not handle nulls when we retrieve data, we could end up getting exceptions. For example, following is the query for checking and handling nulls for the category description. The `where` clause checks for the category, and also checks if `categoryID` is not equal to null. The column value will be null if the column value is returned as `DbNull` from the database.

```
var rowItemsCategories = from cats in categories
join item in items
on cats.Field<int>("CategoryID") equals
item.Field<int>("CategoryID")
```

```
where (int)cats["CategoryID"] == 1
&& !cats.IsNull("CategoryID")
select new
{
   itemID = item.Field<int>("IItemID"),
   category = cats.Field<string>("CategoryName"),
   itmName = item.Field<string>("Name")
};
```

Checking the null value of the column value can be avoided by using the `Field` operator. The `Field` method takes care of checking the null value of the column.

```
var rowsItemsCategories = from cats in categories
join item in items
on cats.Field<int>("CategoryID") equals
item.Field<int>("CategoryID")
where cats.Field<int>("CategoryID") == 1
select new
{
   itemID = item.Field<int>("IItemID"),
   category = cats.Field<string>("CategoryName"),
   itmName = item.Field<string>("Name")
};
```

In addition to handling null values, the `Field` operator provides access to the column values of the DataRows.

SetField<T>

This method is used to set the value of DataColumns in DataRows. The advantage here is that we do not have to worry about null values in the `DataSet`.

```
public static void SetField ( this DataRow first,
   System.Data.DataColumn column, T value);
```

Both `Field` and `SetField` are generic methods that do not require casting of the return type. The name of the column specified by `Field` and `SetField` should match the name of the column in `DataSet`, otherwise the `ArgumentException` will be thrown.

Projection

LINQ provides a `select` method for projecting each element of a sequence. Following is an example of the projection applied to the `Categories` table.

```
var tblCategories = db.Categories.AsEnumerable();
var qqry = tblCategories.Select(category => new { cID = category.
```

```
CategoryID, cCategory = category.Category, cDesc = category.
Description })
OrderBy(e => e.cCategory);
foreach (var cats in qqry)
{
   Console.WriteLine("Id:" + cats.cID + "   Desc:" + cats.cDesc);
}
```

The query, qqry, is built by the projection operator on the Categories table. The select method projects DataColumn elements into a new form of DataRows. The OrderBy operator is applied on the Category DataColumn, which is responsible for ordering the resultant data rows.

Join

This is an operator that joins the elements of two different sequences based on the matching keys. This is similar to the join operator that we have in database queries. The following example has two different tables, tblCategoriesforJoin and tblItemsforJoins having a common DataColumn. The join can be applied on the key column CategoryID of both the sequences.

```
var tblCategoriesforJoin = dataSetDeserts.Tables[0].AsEnumerable();
var tblItemsforJoins = dataSetDeserts.Tables[1].AsEnumerable();
var categoryItems = tblCategoriesforJoin.Join(tblItemsforJoins, o =>
o.Field<int>("CategoryID"), c => c.Field<int>
("CategoryID"),(c, o) => new
{
   CategoryID = c.Field<int>("CategoryID"),
   ItemID = o.Field<int>("IItemID"),
   Name = o.Field<string>("Name")
});
foreach (var itm in categoryItems)
{
   Console.WriteLine("CategoryID:" + itm.CategoryID + "   ItemID:" +
                  itm.ItemID + "   Name:" + itm.Name);
}
```

A join is applied on the first DataTable. It takes four parameters: name of the other table, which participates in the join; outerKeySelector; innerKeySelector; and the actual result of the join operation.

SequenceEqual

This operator is used for comparing two different sequences. It returns a boolean value, which says yes or no. It takes only one argument, which is the second set of enumerable DataRows. Following is an example for checking the equality of two different sequences, `tblCategoriesforJoin` and `tblItemsforJoins`.

```
var categoryItems =
    tblCategoriesforJoin.SequenceEqual(tblItemsforJoins);
```

Skip

This operator is useful when we want to skip some of the rows from a DataTable. For example the following statement shows a way to skip the first two rows from the `tblCategoriesforJoin` table.

```
var categoryItems2 = tblCategoriesforJoin.Skip(2);
```

Apart from the operators covered so far in this chapter, there are many other operators which can be applied on `DataTables` and `DataSets` for querying, such as `SelectMany()`, `Reverse()`, `Sum()`, `ToList()`, `TakeWhile()`, and so on.

Distinct

This `Distinct` operator produces a distinct set of rows from a given sequence of rows. It removes repeated rows from a set. The result is an enumerable DataTable which contains distinct DataRows from the source table. For example, the following code produces distinct rows from the `Categories` table. If it contains any duplicate rows, they will be removed and the resultant table will not have any duplication.

```
var distinctCategories = categories.Distinct();
```

Summary

In this chapter, we saw different ways of taking advantage of LINQ to query `DataRows` in typed, as well as un-typed, `DataSets`. We have also seen different DataSet-specific query operators that make it easier to query `DataRow` objects. Some of these operators are not only used for comparing a sequence of rows, but also for accessing the column values of `DataRows`. In addition, we have seen some of the queries used for querying a single table in a `DataSet`, as well as multiple tables. So LINQ to DataSet makes it easier and faster to query cached data. Queries are not represented as string literals in the code; instead, they are the programming language itself. LINQ also provides compile time syntax checking, static typing and IntelliSense support, which increases a developer's productivity.

6
LINQ to XSD

LINQ to XSD enhances XML programming by adding the feature of typed views on un-typed XML trees. A similar type of feature is available for DataSets in ADO. NET programming where we have typed DataSets. LINQ to XSD gives a better programming environment by providing the object models generated from XML schemas. This is called **typed XML programming**.

LINQ to XSD is an incubation project on typed XML programming. This product is not released yet. All examples and information in this chapter are based on this incubation project and are tested with Visual Studio 2008 Beta 1.

This LINQ to XSD project should reference `System.Xml.XLinq` and `Microsoft.Xml.Schema.Linq` libraries. Following is an example of accessing un-typed XML elements using LINQ query.

```
from c in LoadIcecreams.Elements("Icecream")
select new XElement("Icecream",
c.Element("Price"),
c.Element("Name")));
```

An equivalent LINQ query for the above un-typed XML as a typed XML would be as follows:

```
from Icecream in chapter6.Icecream
select new {Icecream.Price, Icecream.Name};
```

In this chapter we will see how to create typed XML, the features supported by typed XML, and how it helps in development.

The XML element that has been assigned a data type in an XML schema is called typed XML. This data type is used by the XML parser to validate the XML element value against the data type. The data type definition resides either in the same XML file, or in a separate schema file.

Let us consider the following XML in all our examples. It contains a namespace called `http://www.Sample.com/Items`. The XML has details of three different ice-creams. The root element of the XML is `Chapter6`. The first line in the XML shows details like version, and encoding for the XML.

```xml
<?xml version="1.0" encoding="utf-8"?>
<Chapter6 xmlns="http://www.Sample.com/Items">
  <Icecream>
    <!--Chocolate Fudge Icecream-->
    <Name>Chocolate Fudge Icecream</Name>
    <Type>Chocolate</Type>
    <Ingredients>cream, milk, sugar, corn syrup, cellulose gum...</
Ingredients>
    <Cholestrol>50mg</Cholestrol>
    <TotalCarbohydrates>35g</TotalCarbohydrates>
    <Price>10.5</Price>
    <Protein>
      <VitaminA>3g</VitaminA>
      <Calcium>1g</Calcium>
      <Iron>1g</Iron>
    </Protein>
    <TotalFat>
      <SaturatedFat>9g</SaturatedFat>
      <TransFat>11g</TransFat>
    </TotalFat>
  </Icecream>
  <Icecream>
    <!--Cherry Vanilla Icecream-->
    <Name>Vanilla Icecream</Name>
    <Type>Vanilla</Type>
    <Ingredients>vanilla extract, guar gum, cream, nonfat milk, sugar,
locust bean gum, carrageenan, annatto color...</Ingredients>
    <Cholestrol>65mg</Cholestrol>
    <TotalCarbohydrates>26g</TotalCarbohydrates>
    <Price>9.5</Price>
    <Protein>
      <VitaminA>1g</VitaminA>
      <Calcium>2g</Calcium>
      <Iron>1g</Iron>
    </Protein>
    <TotalFat>
      <SaturatedFat>7g</SaturatedFat>
      <TransFat>9g</TransFat>
    </TotalFat>
```

```
    </Icecream>
    <Icecream>
      <!-- Chocolate Icecream-->
      <Name>Banana Split Chocolate Icecream</Name>
      <Type>Chocolate</Type>
      <Ingredients>Banana, guar gum, cream, nonfat milk, sugar, alomnds,
raisins, honey, locust bean gum, chocolate, annatto color...</
Ingredients>
      <Cholestrol>58mg</Cholestrol>
      <TotalCarbohydrates>24g</TotalCarbohydrates>
      <Price>11</Price>
      <Protein>
        <VitaminA>2g</VitaminA>
        <Calcium>1g</Calcium>
        <Iron>1g</Iron>
      </Protein>
      <TotalFat>
        <SaturatedFat>7g</SaturatedFat>
        <TransFat>6g</TransFat>
      </TotalFat>
    </Icecream>
  </Chapter6>
```

Un-typed XML

Following is a sample query for accessing data from an un-typed XML, shown pereviously:

```
XNamespace ns = "http://www.sample.com/Items";
return
(
  from icecreams in Items.Elements(ns + "Icecreams")
  from item in icecreams.Elements(ns + "Icecream")
  select item.Element(ns + "Price"),
  item.Element(ns + "Name")
);
```

The query uses a namespace, ns. This namespace is used to uniquely identify the XML elements. It is prefixed with all the elements used in the query. Each element of the XML is accessed using Element object. The select statement in the query above uses Element object to access the value of Price and Name of each Icecream in the XML document.

Typed XML

The following code is the XML Schema (XSD) contract for the sample XML that we have in the previous section. This schema defines a namespace for the XML, a type for the XML element and its maximum and minimum occurrences. It also describes the name and type for each element in the XML.

```xml
<?xml version="1.0" encoding="utf-8" ?>
<xs:schema id="IcecreamsSchema"
  targetNamespace="http://www.Sample.com/Items"
  elementFormDefault="qualified"
  xmlns="http://www.Sample.com/Items"
  xmlns:mstns="http://www.Sample.com/Items"
  xmlns:xs="http://www.w3.org/2001/XMLSchema">

<xs:element name="Chapter6">
  <xs:complexType>
    <xs:sequence>
      <xs:element ref="Icecream"
                  minOccurs="0" maxOccurs="unbounded"/>
    </xs:sequence>
  </xs:complexType>
</xs:element>
<xs:element name="Icecream">
  <xs:complexType>
    <xs:sequence>
      <xs:element name="Name" type="xs:string"/>
      <xs:element name="Type" type="xs:string"/>
      <xs:element name="Ingredients" type="xs:string"/>
      <xs:element name="Cholestrol" type="xs:string"/>
      <xs:element name="TotalCarbohydrates" type="xs:string"/>
      <xs:element name="Price" type="xs:double"/>
      <xs:element ref="Protein"
                  minOccurs="0" maxOccurs="1"/>
      <xs:element ref="TotalFat"
                  minOccurs="0" maxOccurs="1"/>
    </xs:sequence>
  </xs:complexType>
</xs:element>
<xs:element name="Protein">
  <xs:complexType>
    <xs:sequence>
      <xs:element name="VitaminA" type="xs:string"/>
      <xs:element name="Calcium" type="xs:string"/>
      <xs:element name="Iron" type="xs:string"/>
    </xs:sequence>
  </xs:complexType>
</xs:element>
<xs:element name="TotalFat">
```

```
    <xs:complexType>
      <xs:sequence>
        <xs:element name="SaturatedFat" type="xs:string"/>
        <xs:element name="TransFat" type="xs:string"/>
      </xs:sequence>
    </xs:complexType>
  </xs:element>
</xs:schema>
```

LINQ to XSD automatically creates classes from the XML schema used for the XML. These classes provide typed views of XML elements. Instances of LINQ to XSD types are referred to as **XML Objects**. Instances of LINQ to XSD classes are wrappers-around instances of the LINQ to XML class, `XElement`. All LINQ to XSD classes have a common base class, `XTypedElement`. This is contained in the `Microsoft.Xml.Schema.Lin` library.

```
public class XTypedElement
{
  private XElement xElement;
  /*
    Remaining class definition
  */
}
```

The element declaration is mapped to a subclass of `XTypedElement`, shown as follows:

```
public class Icecream : XTypedElement
  {
      //
  }
```

These classes contain a default constructor, and properties for the elements and attributes. It also provides methods like `Load`, `Save`, `Clone`, etc. When XML is typed, the XML tree is readily loaded into the instance of the generated classes. Here, the type casting of the elements is not required for querying the XML elements.

Creating Typed XML using Visual Studio

Visual Studio gives IDE support for the LINQ to XSD feature. It automates the mapping of schemas to classes. The following example is based on LINQ to XSD, Preview Alpha 2.0 with Visual Studio Beta 1.

Using the **New Project** option, create a **LINQ to XSD Console Application**.

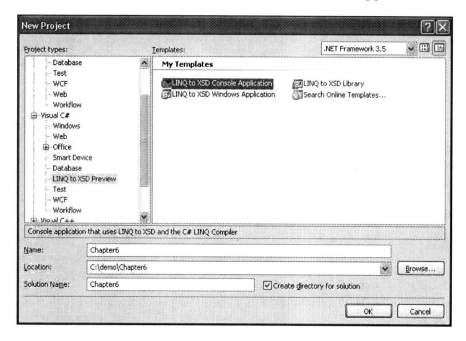

Using the **Add New Item** dialog, select the option to create an XML file under the project. If you have an XML file already, add it to the project using **Add Existing Item** option or copy-paste the contents of the available XML into the new XML file that is added to the project.

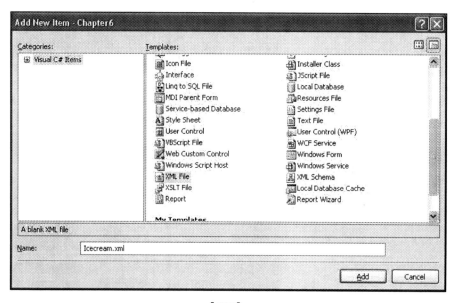

Similarly add the XML schema file to the project. After adding the schema file, copy the schema content given in the typed XML section into the file.

Now we have an XML file and an XML schema file, but we need a tool to generate an object model for the schema. Open the **Properties** window of the XML schema file and select **LinqToXsdSchema** under **Build Action**. This is to instruct the tool to consider the schema file in its build process.

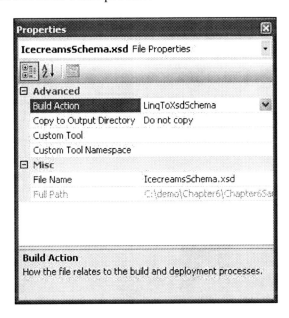

The object model for the XML schema will get generated only after the build process. This build process also enables the IntelliSense for the generated classes, and also displays the information in the **Object Browser** window. To view the object browser, select the menu option **View | Object Browser** from the Visual Studio IDE. This will display the hierarchy of all the objects present in the current project.

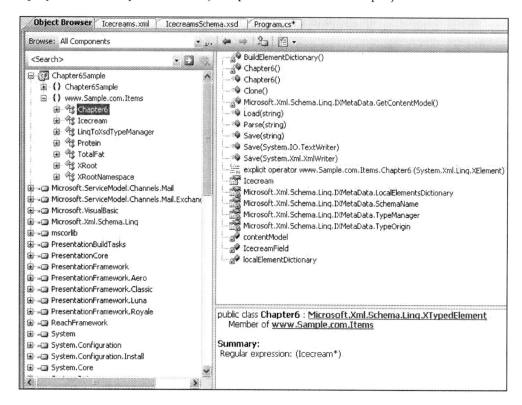

Now we can code with objects using IntelliSense, as shown in the following screenshot:

```csharp
using System;
using System.Linq;
using System.Collections.Generic;
using System.Text;
using System.Xml;
using System.Xml.Linq;
using www.Sample.com;
using www.Sample.com.Items;
```
```
                       {} Items    namespace www.Sample.com.Items
```
```csharp
namespace Chapter6Sample
{
    class Program
    {
```

We can also get a list of objects with the use of IntelliSense, as shown in the following screenshot:

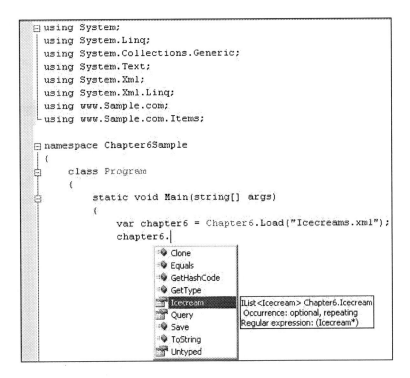

Object Construction

LINQ to XML provides a powerful feature called **functional construction**, which is the ability to create an XML tree in a single statement. All attributes and elements are listed as arguments of XElement constructor. XElement constructor takes various types of arguments for content. The argument can be an XElement, XAttribute, or an array of objects, so that we can pass any number of objects to the XElement. The functional construction feature is mainly used for navigating and modifying the elements and attributes of an XML tree. It actually transforms one form of data into another, instead of manipulating it.

The following code shows how to build an un-typed XML tree using functional construction. Here, we use XElement to build a new Icecream element and add it to the existing Icecream element. For adding each element, we have to use XElement with the element name and value as parameters.

```
Icecream.Add
(
new XElement("Icecream",
new XElement("Name", "Rum Raisin Ice Cream"),
new XElement("Ingredients", "Rum, guar gum, nonfat milk, cream,
alomnds,
    sugar, raisins, honey, chocolate, annatto color..."),
new XElement("Cholesterol", "49mg"),
new XElement("TotalCarbohydrates", "28g"),
new XElement("Protein",
new XElement("VitaminA", "2g"),
new XElement("Calcium", "1g"),
new XElement("Iron", "4g")),
new XElement("TotalFat", "16g",
new XElement("SaturatedFat", "5g"),
new XElement("TransFat", "3g"))
)
);
```

Now we will see how to add a new element to the typed XML, without using XElement. We can directly use the objects to add the elements.

```
var newObj = new Icecream
{
  Name = "Rum Raisin Ice Cream",
  Ingredients = "Rum, guar gum, nonfat milk, cream, alomnds, sugar,
  raisins, honey, chocolate, annatto color...",
  Cholestrol = "49mg",
  TotalCarbohydrates = "28g",
  Protein = new Protein {VitaminA = "2g", Iron = "4g",
    Calcium = "1g"},
  Price = 10.25,
  TotalFat = new TotalFat {SaturatedFat = "5g", TransFat = "3g"}
};
chapter6.Icecream.Add(newObj);
```

Load Method

This is similar to the `Load` method that we saw for LINQ to XML, but the difference is that the `Load` method here is the typed version of the LINQ to XML's `Load` method. Below is a sample which loads the xml file.

```
var chapter6 = Chapter6.Load("Icecreams.xml");
```

Here `chapter6` is a specific type which is already defined. The un-typed loading in LINQ to XML can be made typed by casting the un-typed loading with the type that is required.

In this example, you can see the casting of `Chapter6` done to the `XElement`, used for loading the XML document into `chapterSix`, which is a variable equivalent to the typed XML, `chapter6`.

Parse Method

This method is the typed version of the `Parse` method used in LINQ to XML. Parsing is used to convert a string containing XML into `XElement` and cast that instance to a type required. Following is an example which parses a string containing XML, and types it to `Chapter6`.

```
var chapter6Parse = Chapter6.Parse( " <Chapter6 xmlns='http://www.
Sample.com/Items'> <Icecream> " +
" <!--Chocolate Fudge Icecream--> " +
" <Name>Chocolate Fudge Icecream</Name> "+
" <Type>Chocolate</Type> "+
" <Ingredients>cream, milk, sugar, corn syrup, cellulose gum...</
Ingredients> " +
" <Cholestrol>50mg</Cholestrol> " +
" <TotalCarbohydrates>35g</TotalCarbohydrates>" +
" <Price>10.5</Price> " +
" <Protein> " +
"        <VitaminA>3g</VitaminA> " +
```

```
"          <Calcium>1g</Calcium> " +
"          <Iron>1g</Iron> " +
" </Protein> " +
" <TotalFat> " +
"          <SaturatedFat>9g</SaturatedFat> " +
"          <TransFat>11g</TransFat> " +
" </TotalFat> " +
" </Icecream></Chapter6> "
);
```

Save Method

This method is the typed version of the `Save` method used by LINQ to XML. This
method outputs the XML tree as a file, a `TextWriter`, or an `XmlWriter`.

```
// Save as xml file
  chapter6.Save(@"c:\LINQtoXSDSave.xml");
// or output as TextWriter
  chapter6.Save(TextWriter testTextWriter);
// or output as XmlWriter
  chapter6.Save(XmlWriter testXmlWriter);
```

The above code saves the XML tree in `chapter6` object to a file named
`LINQtoXSDSave.xml`.

Clone Method

The `XTypedElement` base class used for all the generated classes defines a `Clone`
method. The result of the clone operation is weakly typed, as the clone is applied to
the underlying un-typed XML tree. So, to get a specific type, a casting must be used
while cloning.

```
// Load xml
var chapter6 = Chapter6.Load("Icecreams.xml");
// Create a Clone of chapter6 xml
var chapter6Clone = (Chapter6)chapter6.Clone();
var Qry1 = from Icecream in chapter6Clone.Icecream
select new { Icecream.Price, Icecream.Name };
Console.WriteLine(" ");
Console.WriteLine("Clone Sample ");
foreach (var itm in Qry1)
  Console.WriteLine("Price of {0} is : {1}", itm.Name , itm.Price);
```

In the above example, we are loading the XML into `chapter6` variable, and then creating a clone for it. We are type casting the new clone of the type `Chapter6`, and then assigning the resultant clone to `chapter6Clone`. Even though we have not assigned any XML to `chapter6Clone`, the query produces the same result as that of the same query applied on `chapter6` XML. Internally, the XML is the same for both objects, as `chapter6Clone` is just a clone of `chapter6`.

Default Values

Default is the value returned for the elements in the XML, in case the value of the XML element is empty in the XML tree. The same applies to the attributes also, but in case of attributes, they may not be present in the XML tree. The default value is specified in the XML fragment.

```
<xs:element name="Protein">
  <xs:complexType>
    <xs:sequence>
      <xs:element name="VitaminA" type="xs:string" default="0g"/>
      <xs:element name="Calcium" type="xs:string" default="0g"/>
      <xs:element name="Iron" type="xs:string" default="0g"/>
    </xs:sequence>
  </xs:complexType>
</xs:element>
```

In the above example, the elements `VitaminA`, `Calcium`, and `Iron` are the three elements that have a default value of `0g`. So if the XML tree does not have any value specified for these elements, the resulting value for these elements would be 0g.

Customization of XML Objects

The various types of customizations used in LINQ are explained in the following subsections.

Mapping Time Customization

There is a configuration file that controls the LINQ to XSD mapping details. XML namespaces can be mapped to CLR namespaces. For example, the default mapping for `http://www.Sample.com/Items` would be `www.Sample.com.Items`. The following example maps `http://www.Sample.com/Items` to `LinqToXsdExample.Schema.Items`:

```
<Configuration xmlns="http://www.microsoft.com/xml/schema/linq">
  <Namespaces>
    <Namespace
      Schema="http://www.Sample.com/Items"
```

```
        Clr="LinqToXsdExample.Schema.Items"/>
    </Namespaces>
</Configuration>
```

This is also used for systematic conversion of nested, anonymous complex types into complex type definitions.

A configuration file is:

- An XML file with a designated namespace.
- Used by the command line processor of LINQ to XSD.
- Used in Visual Studio for LINQ to XSD project. The build action can be specified as `LinqToXsdConfiguration`.

We can map the Schema without a target namespace to a CLR namespace.

Compile Time Customization

LINQ to XSD generates classes, and provides the object model which can be customized using .NET. It is not so easy to customize the generated code as it requires a lot of understanding. Even if we customize the generated code, the customization will be lost if the code gets regenerated. The best option is to use sub-classing or extension of `partial` classes by which we can add methods to the generated class by LINQ to XSD.

Following is the object model for our `chapter6` XML where **chapter6**, **Icecream**, **Protein**, and **TotalFat** are all generated as classes.

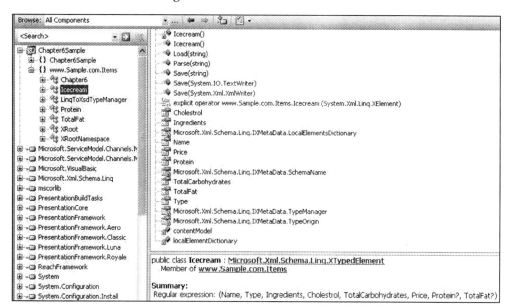

Now we can create a partial class for the corresponding classes, and add methods to override the base class functionality.

The LINQ to XSD Visual Studio projects use the `obj\Debug\LinqToXsdSource.cs` file to hold the generated classes.

Post Compile Customization

For customizing the classes at compile time, we can use partial classes. If the object models are available in compiled format, and we do not have the source for the generated classes, we can use the extension methods to add the behaviour to the compiled objects. The LINQ to XML annotation facility can be used for this.

Using LINQ to XSD at Command Line

There is a command line tool called `LinqToXsd.exe` which is an XSD to class mapper. This tool provides two options to convert XSD:

- Generating a `.dll` from XSD.
- Generating a `.cs` file from XSD, which is a default.

For example, following is the command to generate a DLL from an XSD from the location where the LINQ to XSD is installed:

```
LinqToXsd.exe Items.xsd /lib: Items.dll
```

Summary

In this chapter, we have seen the different features that are going to come up with LINQ to XSD. We have also seen examples for some of the features supported by LINQ to XSD. This makes the programmer's job easier by turning the un-typed XML to typed XML. LINQ to XSD generates the classes for XML elements, and also provides an object model, which the programmer can directly access, just as he or she would do with .NET objects.

7
Standard Query Operators

Standard query operators provide querying capabilities on objects in the .NET Framework. It is a set of methods which can operate on objects whose type implements the `IEnumerable<T>` or `IQueryable<T>` interface. `IEnumerable` exposes the enumerator which iterates over a collection of a specified type. There are different sets of methods that operate on static members of `Enumerable` and `Queryable` classes. Each query can have any number of methods within it. The more number of methods in a query, the more complex it is. The query operators are useable with any .NET language that support generics.

There are some differences in the query execution timings, depending on the value that the query returns. If the query returns a single value, like an average or a sum, it executes immediately and returns the value. If it is a sequence of values, the query would be deferred and would return an enumerable object.

In this chapter we will see types of standard query operators provided by LINQ and how we can use some of those against different data sources.

Whenever we create a new project, we get default namespaces added to the project. The namespace that takes care of importing the query operators is:

```
using System.Linq;
```

We shall see examples of some of these query operators that are used in many applications. Before going into the details of operators, we have to define the classes and objects on which we can apply the queries. We will create the following classes in our project.

```
public class Categories
{
   public string Category {Get; Set;}
   public string Description {Get; Set;}
}
public class Item
{
   public string Category {Get; Set;}
   public string Name {Get; Set;}
   public string Ingredients {Get; Set;}
   public string TotalFat {Get; Set;}
   public string Cholesterol {Get; Set;}
   public string TotalCarbohydrates {Get; Set;}
   public string Protein {Get; Set;}
   public double Price {Get; Set;}
   public FatContent FatContents {Get; Set;}
}
public class FatContent
{
   public string SaturatedFat {Get; Set;}
   public string TransFat {Get; Set;}
   public string OtherFat {Get; Set;}
}
```

The `Categories` class holds different categories of items like ice-creams and pastries. The `Items` class contains the properties that hold information about different catagories. The third class, `FatContent`, holds detailed information about fat content in each item.

Following is a table that lists operators provided by LINQ:

Operators	Description
Aggregation operators	Aggregation operators are used to compute a single value from a collection of values. For example, getting the average or sum of numbers from the collection.
Projection operators	Projection operators are useful for transforming elements.
Concatenation operators	This operator performs the operation of concatenating one sequence to another.
Element operators	Element operators return a single element from a sequence of elements. For example, returning the first, last, or an element at a specific index from a list.
Conversion operators	These operators change the type of the input object.

Operators	Description
Equality operators	These operators check for equality of two sequences. For example, two sequences having the same number of elements are considered equal.
Generation operators	These operators are used for generating a new sequence of values.
Grouping operators	These operators are for grouping elements together that share a common attribute.
Join operators	These operators are used to associate objects from one data source with objects in another data source, based on a common attribute.
Partitioning operators	These operators are used to divide an input sequence into two or more sections, and then return the one section that is required.
Quantifiers	These operators perform the operation of checking whether some or all of the elements in a sequence satisfy a condition.
Restriction operators	These operators restrict the query result to contain elements that satisfy the specific condition.
Set operators	This is to get the result sets based on the presence or absence of equivalent elements in the same or another collection.
Ordering operators	These operators are used for ordering elements in a sequence based on one or more attributes. We can also specify the order within the group of elements to be sorted.

Restriction Operators

Filtering is an operation to restrict the result of a query to contain elements that satisfy a specific condition. We will cover restriction operators in detail in the following sub-sections.

Where

The Where operator filters a sequence, and the declaration would be as follows:

For IEnumerable elements:

```
public static IEnumerable<TSource> Where<TSource>
(
    IEnumerable<TSource> source,
    Func<TSource, bool> predicate
)
```

For `IQueryable` elements:

```
public static IQueryable<TResult> OfType<TResult>
(
    IQueryable source
)
```

The `Where` operator returns an enumerable object from the arguments passed in. When the returned object is enumerated, the enumeration takes places on the sequence and returns those elements for which the predicate function returns true. In the above declaration, the first argument is the source to be tested and the second argument is optional, and if present it represents the elements in the source.

The following example returns the items with price less than 10.

```
IEnumerable<Item> lowPricedItems =
from item in items
where item.Price < 10
select item;
```

An equivalent translation for the previous query, is given as follows:

```
IEnumerable<Item> itemsWithLessPrice = items.
Where(I => I.Price < 10);
```

The following example shows the usage of the `IQueryable` method to filter elements in a sequence.

```
IQueryable<Item> qryItemsWithLessPrice = items.AsQueryable().
Where(I => I.Price < 10);
```

If the source or predicate is null in the `Where` clause, then an `ArgumentNullException` will be thrown.

OfType

This operator filters elements based on the type of elements in the collection. Following is a list that contains different objects, like `String` and `Icecreams`, within the same `ArrayList`:

```
private static ArrayList GetStringsandIcecreams()
{
    System.Collections.ArrayList arrList = new
    System.Collections.ArrayList(4);
        arrList.Add("String value One");
        arrList.Add("String value Two");
        arrList.Add("String value Three");
```

```
    arrList.Add(new Icecreams
                {Category="Icecreams", Name="Chocolate
                    Fudge Icecream", Ingredients="cream, milk,
                    mono and diglycerides...",
                    Cholesterol="50mg", Protein="4g",
                    TotalCarbohydrates="35g",
                    TotalFat="20g", Price=10.5
                });
    arrList.Add(new Icecreams
                {Category="Icecreams", Name="Vanilla Icecream",
                    Ingredients="vanilla extract, guar gum, cream...",
                    Cholesterol="65mg", Protein="4g",
                    TotalCarbohydrates="26g", TotalFat="16g",
Price=9.80});
    return arrList;
}
```

Now from this list, if we want to get a list of strings, we can use the `OfType` operator to filter the objects.

```
ArrayList arrList = GetStringsandIcecreams();
// Apply OfType() to the ArrayList.
IEnumerable<string> query1 = arrList.OfType<string>();
Console.WriteLine("Elements of type 'string' are:");
foreach (string str in query1)
Console.WriteLine(str);
```

If we want to extract the objects of type `Icecream` from the list, we filter for the `Icecream` object.

```
// Call the type OfType() and then the Where() operator
// to filter the types from the list with a condition
IEnumerable<Icecreams> query2 =
arrList.OfType<Icecreams>().Where(icecrms => icecrms.Name.
Contains("Vanilla Icecream"));
Console.WriteLine("\nThe Icecream object that contains the name
                    'Vanilla Icecream':");
foreach (Icecreams ice in query2)
Console.WriteLine(ice.Name);
```

Projection Operators

These operators are used for transforming one form of elements into another. For example, we can project one or two properties of an object to create a new type. We can also project the original object without any change. We will cover projection operators in detail in the following sub-sections:

Select

This `select` operator is implemented using deferred execution. This query gets executed only when the return object in the query is enumerated using looping statements or by calling the enumeration methods. The enumeration happens by calling the `GetEnumerator` method, which is called implicitly when using the `foreach` loop. Shown below are the syntaxes for using the `select` operator.

```
public static IEnumerable<TResult> Select<TSource, TResult>
(
    IEnumerable<TSource> source,
    Func<TSource, TResult> selector
)

public static IQueryable<TResult> Select<TSource, TResult>
(
    IQueryable<TSource> source,
    Expression<Func<TSource, TResult>> selector
)
```

The first argument is the element to process and the second argument represents the index of the element in the source of the first argument. The element returned from the selector method could be an object or a collection. If it is a collection, the programmer has to take care of reading the collection and returning the values.

The following example creates a sequence of the names of all items:

```
IEnumerable<string> icecreamNames = items.Select(itm => itm.Name);
```

Following is an equivalent query of the above expression:

```
IEnumerable<string> icecreamsNames = from itm in items
select itm.Name;
```

The following code returns items with a price less than 10:

```
IEnumerable<Item> lowPricedItems =
from item in items
where item.Price < 10
select item;
```

```
Console.WriteLine("Items with low price:");
foreach (var item in lowPricedItems)
{
    Console.WriteLine("Price of {0} is {1} ", item.Name, item.Price);
}
```

The following expression is another example to retrieve items and their prices where the price is less than 10:

```
var IcecreamsPrices = items.Where(itm => itm.Price < 10)
.Select(itm => new { itm.Name, itm.Price })
.ToList();
foreach (var ices in IcecreamsPrices)
{
    Console.WriteLine("The price of {0} is {1}", ices.
    Name, ices.Price);
}
```

If the source or the selector in the above methods is null then exception of type `ArgumentNullException` will be thrown.

SelectMany

The `SelectMany` operator performs a one-to-many projection on sequences. This operator enumerates the source and maps each element to an enumerable object. It also enumerates these enumerable objects, and retrieves elements. The first argument is the source element to process, and if the second element is preset, then it represents the elements within the source sequence.

The syntaxes for using the `SelectMany` operator are as follows:

```
public static IEnumerable<TResult> SelectMany<TSource, TResult>
(
    IEnumerable<TSource> source,
    Func<TSource, IEnumerable<TResult>> selector
)

public static IQueryable<TResult> SelectMany<TSource, TResult>
(
    IQueryable<TSource> source,
    Expression<Func<TSource, IEnumerable<TResult>>> selector
)
```

The following code example shows how to use `SelectMany` to perform a one-to-many projection. Let us define a new item object with properties including a list, which contains the list of ingredients for the item.

```
public class NewItem
{
  public string Category { get; set; }
  public string Name { get; set; }
  public List<string> Ingredients { get; set; }
  public double Price { get; set; }
}
```

Now define a method to create a list of items using the new object.

```
private static List<NewItem> GetNewItemsList()
{
  List<NewItem> itemsList = new List<NewItem> {
  new NewItem
  {
    Category="Icecreams", Name="Chocolate Fudge Icecream",
    Ingredients = new List<string> {"cream", "milk", "mono and
                                 diglycerides"},
    Price=10.5
  },
  new NewItem
  {
    Category="Icecreams", Name="Vanilla Icecream",
    Ingredients= new List<string> {"vanilla extract", "guar gum",
                                 "cream"},
    Price=9.80
  },
  new NewItem
  {
    Category="Icecreams", Name="Banana Split Icecream",
    Ingredients= new List<string> {"Banana", "guar gum", "cream"},
    Price=7.5
  }
};
  return itemsList;
}
```

In the above method you can see a list of strings, `Ingredients`, within the `itemsList`. Now using the `SelectMany` operator, collect all the distinct `Ingredients` required for all items.

```
List<NewItem> itemss = GetNewItemsList();
IEnumerable<string> ingredients = itemss.
SelectMany(ing => ing.Ingredients);
Console.WriteLine("List of all Ingredients for the Icecreams");
foreach (string str in ingredients.Distinct())
{
   Console.WriteLine(str);
}
```

The output of this code would be a collection of ingredients for each item.

Join Operators

A join is an association of objects from different data sources that share a common attribute. These operators perform the same operations that are performed by the database queries. Each data source will have certain key attributes by which we can compare the values, and collect information. The different join operators are covered in detail in the following sub-sections.

Join

This operator joins two sequences, based on matching keys extracted from elements in sequences.

```
public static IEnumerable<TResult> Join<TOuter, TInner, TKey, TResult>
(
   IEnumerable<TOuter> outer,
   IEnumerable<TInner> inner,
   Func<TOuter, TKey> outerKeySelector,
   Func<TInner, TKey> innerKeySelector,
   Func<TOuter, TInner, TResult> resultSelector
)
public static IQueryable<TResult> Join<TOuter, TInner, TKey, TResult>
(
   IQueryable<TOuter> outer,
   IEnumerable<TInner> inner,
   Expression<Func<TOuter, TKey>> outerKeySelector,
   Expression<Func<TInner, TKey>> innerKeySelector,
   Expression<Func<TOuter, TInner, TResult>> resultSelector
)
```

The IEqualityComparer is used to compare keys. This is shown in the following code:

```
public static IEnumerable<TResult> Join<TOuter, TInner,
  TKey, TResult>
(
  IEnumerable<TOuter> outer,
  Enumerable<TInner> inner,
  Func<TOuter, TKey> outerKeySelector,
  Func<TInner, TKey> innerKeySelector,
  Func<TOuter, TInner, TResult> resultSelector,
  IEqualityComparer<TKey> comparer
)
public static IQueryable<TResult> Join<TOuter, TInner, TKey, TResult>
(
  IQueryable<TOuter> outer,
  IEnumerable<TInner> inner,
  Expression<Func<TOuter, TKey>> outerKeySelector,
  Expression<Func<TInner, TKey>> innerKeySelector,
  Expression<Func<TOuter, TInner, TResult>> resultSelector,
  IEqualityComparer<TKey> comparer
)
```

This is similar to inner join in relation database terms. These operators join two different sequences and collect common information from the sequences with the help of matching keys in the sequences. The outerKeySelector and innerKeySelector arguments specify functions that extract the join key values from elements of the outer and inner sequences, respectively. The resultSelector argument specifies a function that creates a result element from two matching outer and inner sequence elements. It first enumerates the inner sequence and collects the elements and their keys using innerKeySelector. It then enumerates the outer sequence to collect the elements and their keys using the outerKeySelector function. Using these selections, the resultSelector is evaluated for the resulting sequence. It also maintains the order of the elements in sequences.

The following code is an example for joining categories with items having category as the key between these two sequences. The result is a combination of categories, items, and ingredients.

```
List<Item> items = GetItemsList();
List<Categories> categories = GetCategoriesList();
var CategoryItems = categories.Join(items,
category => category.Category,
item => item.Category,
(category, item) => new { Category = category.Category, Item =
```

```
item.Name, Ingr = item.Ingredients });
foreach (var str in CategoryItems)
{
  Console.WriteLine("{0} - {1} - {2}", str.Category, str.Item,
    str.Ingr);
}
```

Following is an equivalent query for the example above:

```
List<Item> items = GetItemsList();
List<Categories> categories = GetCategoriesList();
var CategoryItemJoin = from Cat in categories
join Itm in items on Cat.Category equals Itm.Category
select new { Cat.Category, Itm.Name, Itm.Ingredients };
Console.WriteLine("Join using Query :");
foreach (var elements in CategoryItemJoin)
{
  Console.WriteLine("{0} - {1} - {2}", elements.Category,
    elements.Name, elements.Ingredients);
}
```

An `ArgumentNullException` is thrown if any of the argument is null.

GroupJoin

The `GroupJoin` operator groups the results of a join between two sequences based on equality of keys. The default equality comparer is used to compare keys.

```
public static IEnumerable<TResult> GroupJoin<TOuter, TInner, TKey,
  TResult>
(
  IEnumerable<TOuter> outer,
  IEnumerable<TInner> inner,
  Func<TOuter, TKey> outerKeySelector,
  Func<TInner, TKey> innerKeySelector,
  Func<TOuter, IEnumerable<TInner>, TResult> resultSelector
)
public static IEnumerable<TResult> GroupJoin<TOuter, TInner, TKey,
  TResult>
(
  IEnumerable<TOuter> outer,
  IEnumerable<TInner> inner,
  Func<TOuter, TKey> outerKeySelector,
  Func<TInner, TKey> innerKeySelector,
  Func<TOuter, IEnumerable<TInner>, TResult> resultSelector,
  IEqualityComparer<TKey> comparer
)
```

All the arguments are very similar to those we saw under the `Join` operator. The `resultSelector` function is called only once for each outer element together with a collection of all the inner elements that match the outer elements. This differs from the `Join` operator, in which the result selector function is invoked on pairs that contain one element from outer and one element from inner. This is similar to the inner joins and left outer joins in relational database terms.

The following code is an example of grouping items under various categories:

```
List<Item> items = GetItemsList();
List<Categories> categories = GetCategoriesList();
var categoriesAndItems = categories.GroupJoin(items,
category => category.Category,
item => item.Category,
(category, categoryItems) => new { Category = category.Category,
Items = categoryItems.Select(item => item.Name) });
foreach (var value in categoriesAndItems)
{
  Console.WriteLine("{0} : ", value.Category);
  foreach (string nam in value.Items)
  {
    Console.WriteLine("     {0} ", nam);
  }
}
```

The same group join can also be achieved through the following query. In this case we are grouping the items according to the category and get the total price of all the items under that category. The keyword, `into`, is used here for grouping the result.

```
List<Item> items = GetItemsList();
List<Categories> categories = GetCategoriesList();
var CategoryItemgroup = from Cat in categories
join Itm in items on Cat.Category equals Itm.Category into CustItem
select new { Cat.Category, TotalPrice=CustItem.Sum(prc => prc.Price)};
Console.WriteLine("GroupJoin using Query :");
foreach (var elements in CategoryItemgroup)
{
  Console.WriteLine("{0} - {1} ", elements.Category,
                    elements.TotalPrice);
}
```

An `ArgumentNullException` is thrown if any argument is null.

Concatenation Operator

Concatenation is the operation of appending one sequence to another. Concat is the operator used for concatenating.

Concat

Concatenation operator combines two different collections into one. When the returned object is enumerated, it first enumerates the first sequence yielding the elements and then it enumerates the second sequence and yields the elements in it. Following is the declaration syntax of this operator:

```
public static IEnumerable<TSource> Concat<TSource>
(
   IEnumerable<TSource> first,
   IEnumerable<TSource> second
)
```

Following is the query which uses the concatenating operator to concatenate an item's name, ingredients and price.

```
List<Item> items = GetItemsList();
IEnumerable<string> itemslist =
   items.Select(itm => itm.Name).
   Concat(items.Select(itms => itms.Ingredients)).
   Concat(items.Select(itm => itm.Price.ToString())).
   Distinct();
   foreach (var itms in itemslist)
   {
      Console.WriteLine("{0}", itms);
   }
```

If the first or the second arguments are null, ArgumentNullException is thrown.

Ordering Operators

Ordering operators are useful when we want the result of a select statement in a particular order. The ordering could be ascending or descending. The declaration syntax for ordering operators is given below:

```
public static IOrderedEnumerable<TSource> OrderBy<TSource, TKey>
(
   IEnumerable<TSource> source,
   Func<TSource, TKey> keySelector
)
public static IOrderedEnumerable<TSource>
   OrderByDescending<TSource, TKey>
```

```
(
  IEnumerable<TSource> source,
  Func<TSource, TKey> keySelector
)
ThenBy<TSource, TKey>
(
  IOrderedSequence<TSource> source,
  Func<TSource, TKey> keySelector
)
public static IOrderedSequence<TSource>
  ThenBy<TSource, TKey>
(
  IOrderedSequence<TSource> source,
  Func<TSource, TKey> keySelector,
  IComparer<TKey> comparer
)
public static IOrderedSequence<TSource>
  ThenByDescending<TSource, TKey> (
  IOrderedSequence<TSource> source,
  Func<TSource, TKey> keySelector
)
public static IOrderedSequence<TSource>
  ThenByDescending<TSource, TKey>
(
  IOrderedSequence<TSource> source,
  Func<TSource, TKey> keySelector,
  IComparer<TKey> comparer
)
public static IEnumerable<TSource> Reverse<TSource>
(
  IEnumerable<TSource> source
)
```

All operators can be composed to order a sequence by multiple keys. The initial ordering is done by the first OrderBy or OrderByDescending operator. The second sorting is done by the first ThenBy or ThenByDescending operator. The second ThenBy or ThenByDescending operators forms the third level of sorting and it goes on like this:

```
Source
OrderBy(....)
ThenBy(....)
ThenBy(....)
```

The OrderBy and ThenBy methods establish an ascending ordering while the OrderByDescending and ThenByDescending are used for sorting in descending order. There is an optional comparer for comparing the key values. If no comparer is specified or if the comparer is null, the default comparer is used.

An `ArgumentNullException` is thrown if the `source` or `keySelector` argument is null. All these sorting operators return an enumerable object.

If one of the sorting operators' resultant objects are enumerated, it first enumerates the source and collects the elements. Then evaluates the `keySelector` function once for each element, collecting the key values of `OrderBy` and then sorts the elements according to the collected key values.

```
List<Item> items = GetItemsList();
IEnumerable<Item> itms =
items.OrderBy(itm => itm.Name).
ThenByDescending(itm => itm.Protein).
ThenBy(itm => itm.TotalFat);
foreach (var item in itms)
{
   Console.WriteLine("(Ascending) {0} (ThenByDescending) {1} (ThenBy)
      {2}", item.Name, item.Protein, item.TotalFat);
}
```

This example creates a sequence of all items ordered by item `Name` first, the `Protein` value of item as second in descending order, and the `TotalFat` value, as the third in ascending order.

The previous example is equivalent to the following query:

```
IEnumerable<Item> itmsQry =
from itm in items
orderby itm.Name, itm.Protein descending, itm.TotalFat
select itm;
```

The `Reverse` operator reverses the sequence of elements. When the source object is enumerated, it enumerates the source sequence collecting the elements and then yielding the elements of the source sequence in reverse order.

Consider the same query for selecting the item with some of its elements in the order. Using the same query, the following code shows how we can reverse the name of each item.

```
foreach (var item in itmsQry)
{
   char[] name = item.Name.ToArray().Reverse().ToArray();
   foreach (char cr in name)
   {
      Console.Write(cr + ""); }
      Console.WriteLine();
   }
}
```

If any of the source argument is null, the execution returns `ArgumentNullException`.

Set Operators

Results of set operations are based on the presence or absence of equivalent elements in the same or other collection. For example, the `Distinct` operator removes repeated elements from collections, and the `Union` operator returns a unique union of elements from different collections. The various set operators are explained in detail in the following sub-sections:

Distinct

The `Distinct` operator is used for retrieving distinct elements from a sequence. Following is the declaration of the `Distinct` operator which uses default equality comparer to compare values:

```
public static IEnumerable<TSource> Distinct<TSource>
(
    IEnumerable<TSource> source
)
```

The following declaration the `Distinct` operator, uses the specified `IEqualityComparer<T>` to compare values.

```
public static IEnumerable<TSource> Distinct<TSource>
(
    IEnumerable<TSource> source,
    IEqualityComparer<TSource> comparer
)
```

Following is the sample code for retrieving the categories from a list of items. The actual execution of the operator takes place when the object is enumerated in the looping statement.

```
List<Item> items = GetItemsList();
IEnumerable<string> icecreamNames = items.
    Select(itm => itm.Category).Distinct();
Console.WriteLine("Distinct Icecream categories :");
foreach (var itm in icecreamNames)
{
    Console.WriteLine("{0}", itm);
}
```

If the source is null, and does not contain any values in it, an `ArgumentNullException` will be thrown.

Except

This operator returns the differences between two different sequences. The sequence is the concatenation of items into a single sequence using comma separation. A sequence can contain duplicate values. It can be nested and collapsed. Here, the Except operator is used to returns those elements in the first sequence that do not appear in the second sequence. Also, it does not return those elements in the second sequence that also appear in the first. The declaration of the Except operator using the default comparer is given as follows:

```
public static IEnumerable<TSource> Except<TSource>
(
    IEnumerable<TSource> first,
    IEnumerable<TSource> second
)
```

Following is the declaration of the Except operator using the specified comparer to compare values:

```
public static IEnumerable<TSource> Except<TSource>
(
    IEnumerable<TSource> first,
    IEnumerable<TSource> second,
    IEqualityComparer<TSource> comparer
)
```

Let us consider, we have two collections of strings where the string values present in the second array are also present in the first. The following code shows how to use the Except operator to fetch the values from the first string array whose values are not present in the second array:

```
string[] stringsOne = { "Icecreams", "Pastries", "Buiscuits",
    "Chocolates", "Juices", "Fruits" };
string[] stringsTwo = { "Icecreams", "Pastries" };
IEnumerable<string> stringsOnlyInFirst =
    stringsOne.Except(stringsTwo);
Console.WriteLine("Except Operator Example :");
foreach (string str in stringsOnlyInFirst)
{
    Console.WriteLine("{0}", str);
}
```

If the source does not have any value in it or if the source is null, the operator throws an ArgumentNullException error.

Intersect

This `Intersect` operator returns items that are common two sequences. Given below are the declarations for the `Intersect` operator.

The declaration of the `Intersect` operator, using default comparer, is given below:

```
public static IEnumerable<TSource> Intersect<TSource>
(
    IEnumerable<TSource> first,
    IEnumerable<TSource> second
)
```

The declaration that uses the specified comparer for comparing the values is as follows:

```
public static IEnumerable<TSource> Intersect<TSource>
(
    IEnumerable<TSource> first,
    IEnumerable<TSource> second,
    IEqualityComparer<TSource> comparer
)
```

This operator first fetches the elements from the first sequence and then compares it with the elements present in the second sequence. It keeps the element, if it is also present in the second sequence. In this manner, it compares all the elements of the first sequence with that of the second sequence and then fetches the common ones.

The following code shows an example of fetching the common elements from two sequences using the `Intersect` operator.

```
string[] stringsOne = { "Icecreams", "Pastries", "Buiscuits",
  "Chocolates", "Juices", "Fruits" };
string[] stringsTwo = { "Icecreams", "Pastries"};
IEnumerable<string> stringsOnlyInFirst =
  stringsOne.Intersect(stringsTwo);
Console.WriteLine("Intersect Operator Example :");
foreach (string str in stringsOnlyInFirst)
{
  Console.WriteLine("{0}", str);
}
```

If the source does not have any value, or has a null value, an `ArgumentNullException` is thrown.

Union

The Union operator is for combining the elements of two different sequences. This is useful for collecting distinct values of different sequences. Given below is the declaration for the Union operator, which uses the default equality comparer.

```
public static IEnumerable<TSource> Union<TSource>
(
    IEnumerable<TSource> first,
    IEnumerable<TSource> second
)
```

Following is the declaration of the Union operator which uses the specified equality operator:

```
public static IEnumerable<TSource> Union<TSource>
(
    IEnumerable<TSource> first,
    IEnumerable<TSource> second,
    IEqualityComparer<TSource> comparer
)
```

This operator first enumerates the first sequence and collects the elements. It then enumerates the second sequence and collects the elements that are not collected already. At the end of enumeration, the operator returns all the distinct elements from both the sequences.

Following is an example for collecting the elements from two different sequences:

```
string[] stringsOne = { "Icecreams", "Pastries", "Buiscuits",
    "Chocolates", "Juices", "Fruits" };
string[] stringsTwo = { "Icecreams", "Coffee", "Tea" };
IEnumerable<string> stringsOnlyInFirst =
    stringsOne.Union(stringsTwo);
Console.WriteLine("Union Operator Example :");
foreach (string str in stringsOnlyInFirst)
{
    Console.WriteLine("{0}", str);
}
```

The values returned from this example, will have the Icecreams value returned only once, as it is already there in the first sequence.

If the source does not have any value, or has a null value, an ArgumentNullException will be thrown.

Grouping Operators

This operator is useful for grouping similar elements, based on a common attribute. GroupBy and ToLookUp are operators used for grouping elements together.

GroupBy

This operator groups all the elements in a sequence with a common key. This operator returns a collection of objects, which are grouped, based on a distinct key in a sequence. The order is maintained based on the order of elements in source. Elements in each group are in the same order they appear in source.

GroupBy<(Of TSource, TKey>)(IEnumerable<(Of TSource>), Func<(Of TSource, TKey>))	Groups the elements according to a specified key selector function.
GroupBy<(Of TSource, TKey>)(IEnumerable<(Of TSource>), Func<(Of TSource, TKey>), IEqualityComparer<(Of TKey>))	Groups the elements according to a specified key selector function and compares the keys by using a specified comparer function.
GroupBy<(Of TSource, TKey, TElement>)(IEnumerable<(Of TSource>), Func<(Of TSource, TKey>), Func<(Of TSource, TElement>))	Groups the elements according to a specified key selector function and selects the resulting elements by using a specified function.
GroupBy<(Of TSource, TKey, TElement>) (IEnumerable<(Of TSource>), Func< (Of TSource, TKey>), Func<(Of TSource, TElement>), IEqualityComparer< (Of TKey>))	Groups the elements of a sequence according to a key selector function. The keys are compared by using a comparer function and the resulting elements are selected using a specified function.

The following code is an example that groups the items based on the category using the GroupBy operator.

```
List<Item> items = GetItemsList();
IEnumerable<IGrouping<string, string>> Items = items.
   GroupBy(itm => itm.Category, itm => itm.Name);
foreach (IGrouping<string, string> itm in Items)
{
   Console.WriteLine("{0}", itm.Key);
   foreach (string nam in itm)
   {
      Console.WriteLine("      {0}", nam);
   }
}
```

The following is an equivalent of the previous:

```
IEnumerable<IGrouping<string, string>> CatItems = from Itm in items
group Itm.Name by Itm.Category;
foreach (IGrouping<string, string> itm in CatItems)
{
  Console.WriteLine("{0}", itm.Key);
  foreach (string nam in itm)
  {
    Console.WriteLine("      {0}", nam);
  }
}
```

ToLookup

This operator puts elements into a one-to-many dictionary, based on a key selector function. The functionality of Lookup should not be confused with the dictionary functionality. A dictionary performs a one-to-one mapping of key value pairs, where as, a Lookup is the grouping of keys to a collection of values. Refer to page number 26 for more examples and explanations regarding ToLookup.

Conversion Operators

These conversion operators are mainly used for converting the data type of the input objects. Some of these operators can be used to force immediate query execution, instead of deferring it until enumeration.

AsEnumerable

This operator returns an input as an IEnumerable<T>. It just changes the compile time type of the source. Following is the declaration of the AsEnumerable operator.

```
public static IEnumerable<TSource> AsEnumerable<TSource>
(
  IEnumerable<TSource> source
)
```

In the next example, we define ArrayList, which is a non-generic type. Using the AsEnumerable operator we will try to convert it as an enumerable object.

```
System.Collections.ArrayList arrList = new
System.Collections.ArrayList(4);
arrList.Add("String value One");
arrList.Add("String value Two");
```

```
arrList.Add(new Icecreams {Category="Icecreams", Name="Vanilla
Icecream",
Ingredients="vanilla extract, guar gum, cream...", Cholesterol="65mg",
  Protein="4g", TotalCarbohydrates="26g", TotalFat="16g",
Price=9.80});
  arrList.Add(new Icecreams {Category="Icecreams", Name="Banana Split
  Icecream", Ingredients="Banana, guar gum, cream...",
  Cholesterol="58mg", Protein="6g", TotalCarbohydrates="24g",
 TotalFat="13g", Price=7.5});
```

Now use the AsEnumerable operator against the list of strings retrieved from the main array list.

```
List<string> query1 = arrList.OfType<string>();
IEnumerable<string> qry = query1.AsEnumerable();
Console.WriteLine("Elements of type 'string' are:");
foreach (string str in qry)
  Console.WriteLine(str);
```

Cast

This operator converts the type of the specified element to a different type. The declaration for the Cast operator is given as follows:

```
public static IEnumerable<TResult> Cast<TResult>
(
  IEnumerable source
)
```

Now let us consider an array list containing objects of type Item, which we have seen in our previous examples. The ArrayList operator does not implement IEnumerable<T>. We can use the Cast operator to change the type of the result.

```
ArrayList stringsOne = new ArrayList
{
  new Item
  {
    Category = "Icecreams", Name = "Chocolate Fudge Icecream",
    Ingredients = "cream, milk, mono and diglycerides...",
    Cholesterol = "50mg", Protein = "4g", TotalCarbohydrates = "35g",
    TotalFat = "20g", Price = 10.5,
    FatContents = new FatContent
    {
      SaturatedFat = "6g", TransFat = "4g", OtherFat = "6g"
    }
```

```
  }
};
IEnumerable<Item> icecreamsList = stringsOne.Cast<Item>().
Where(o => o.Category == "Icecreams");
```

`ArgumentNullException` is raised if the source is null. If the source element cannot be cast to the type specified, `InvalidCastException` will be thrown.

OfType

The `OfType` operator is used to filter elements based on a particular type. This operator can be used along with the `Cast` operator to cast the element of a particular type, so that we can avoid `InvalidcastException`.

Following is an array list which contains mixed types of elements. It has strings, integer and double. Out of these values, if we want to extract only the elements that are strings, then we can use the `OfType` operator as given below.

```
ArrayList strings = new ArrayList(5);
strings.Add("Icecreams");
strings.Add("Chocolates");
strings.Add("Pastries");
strings.Add(5);
strings.Add(2.5);
IEnumerable<string> onlyStrings = strings.OfType<string>();
Console.WriteLine("The Elements of type string are :");
foreach (string str in onlyStrings)
   Console.WriteLine(str);
```

We will get the `ArgumentNullException` if the source value is null.

ToArray

The `ToArray` operator is used for converting a collection into an array. The declaration for the `ToArray` operator is as follows:

```
public static TSource[] ToArray<TSource>
(
   IEnumerable<TSource> source
)
```

This operator enumerates the sequence and returns the elements in the form of an array. If the source is null, an `ArgumentNullException` is thrown.

Following is an example that shows how to get the categories of items in an array using the `ToArray` operator.

```
List<Item> items = GetItemsList();
string[] icecreamNames = items.Select(itm =>
itm.Category).Distinct().ToArray();
foreach (string nam in icecreamNames)
   Console.WriteLine(name);
```

ToDictionary

The `ToDictionary` operator creates a dictionary from a given sequence. Following is the declaration of the `ToDictionary` operator.

```
public static Dictionary<TKey, TSource> ToDictionary<TSource, TKey>
(
   IEnumerable<TSource> source,
   Func<TSource, TKey> keySelector
)
public static Dictionary<TKey, TSource> ToDictionary<TSource, TKey>
(
   IEnumerable<TSource> source,
   Func<TSource, TKey> keySelector,
   IEqualityComparer<TKey> comparer
)
public static Dictionary<TKey, TElement>
   ToDictionary<TSource, TKey, TElement>
(
   IEnumerable<TSource> source,
   Func<TSource, TKey> keySelector,
   Func<TSource, TElement> elementSelector
)
public static Dictionary<TKey, TElement>
   ToDictionary<TSource, TKey, TElement>
(
   IEnumerable<TSource> source,
   Func<TSource, TKey> keySelector,
   Func<TSource, TElement> elementSelector,
   IEqualityComparer<TKey> comparer
)
```

The `KeySelector` and `ElementsSelector` functions are useful for creating a key-value pair for the dictionary. If the `ElementSelector` is not specified, the element itself is considered as a value by default.

Following is an example for creating the dictionary from the list of items:

```
List<Icecreams> items = GetItems();
Dictionary<string, Icecreams> icecreamNames = items.
    ToDictionary(itm => itm.Name);
Console.WriteLine("ToDictionary Example: ");
foreach (KeyValuePair<string, Icecreams> ice in icecreamNames)
    Console.WriteLine("Key:{0}, Name:{1}", ice.Key,
                    ice.Value.Ingredients);
```

In the above example, `items` is a list that contains a list of `Icecreams` objects that have different properties such as name, category, ingredients, price, etc. Here, `KeySelector` is a string which is the key for the dictionary, and the object `Icecreams` itself is the element. The resultant dictionary has the item name as a key and the `Item` itself as a value.

An `ArgumentNullException` is thrown if the source, `KeySelector`, `ElementSelector`, or the `key` itself produced by the `KeySelector` is null. An `ArgumentException` is thrown if the `KeySelector` returns the same key for two elements. Key values are compared using a specified comparer, and if it is not specified, the default comparer is used for comparing.

ToList

The `ToList` operator is used for creating the list from the given sequence. It is enumerated through the sequence and returns the elements as a list.

```
public static List<TSource> ToList<TSource>
(
    IEnumerable<TSource> source
)
```

Following is an example that returns the list of item names from strings:

```
string[] strings = { "Icecreams", "Pastries", "Buiscuits",
"Chocolates", "Juices", "Fruits" };
List<string> icecreamsPrices = strings.ToList();
Console.WriteLine("List of items :");
foreach (var icecream in icecreamsPrices)
Console.WriteLine("{0}", icecream);
```

An `ArgumentNullException` is thrown if the source is null.

ToLookup

The ToLookup method returns a lookup which is a one-to-many dictionary that maps the key to a collection of values.

Overloaded List of ToLookup	Description
ToLookup<(Of TSource, TKey>)(IEnumerable<(Of TSource>), Func<(Of TSource, TKey>))	Creates a lookup according to a specified key selector function.
ToLookup<(Of TSource, TKey>)(IEnumerable<(Of TSource>), Func<(Of TSource, TKey>), IEqualityComparer<(Of TKey>))	Creates a lookup according to the specified key selector and the comparer functions.
ToLookup<(Of TSource, TKey, TElement >)(IEnumerable<(Of TSource>), Func<(Of TSource, TKey>), Func<(Of TSource, TElement>))	Creates a lookup according to the specified key selector and element selector functions.
ToLookup<(Of TSource, TKey, TElement >)(IEnumerable<(Of TSource>), Func<(Of TSource, TKey>), Func<(Of TSource, TElement>), IEqualityComparer<(Of TKey>))	Creates a lookup according to the specified key selector, element selector and comparer functions.

This lookup operator is similar to the dictionary but the dictionary returns one-to-one mapping of keys and values. But the lookup returns the one-to-many mapping of key and collections.

Given below is an example that first gets a collection of items of type Icecream. The items collection contains information for a list of different ice-creams and pastries. The look up operator is used for grouping Icecreams and Pastries as the key, and then looking up the items collection for each key.

```
List<Icecreams> items = GetItems();
Lookup<string, string> lookup = items.
ToLookup(p => p.Category, p => p.Name);
Console.WriteLine("Lookup Operator Example :");
foreach (IGrouping<string, string> group in lookup)
{
  Console.WriteLine(group.Key);
  foreach (string str in group)
    Console.WriteLine("    {0}", str);
}
```

The result from the previous code is shown as follows:

```
Lookup Operator Example :
Icecreams
        Chocolate Fudge Icecream
        Vanilla Icecream
        Banana Split Icecream
        Rum Raisin Ice Cream
Pastries
        Black Forest
```

If the source or the key selector is null, `ArgumentNullException` is thrown.

Equality Operators

This is to find the equality between two sequences. They are considered equal if the number of elements and their value are equal. `SequenceEqual` is the operator used for finding the equality between the sequences.

SequenceEqual

This operator is useful for comparing two sequences and finding their equality. This operator compares the elements in two sequences by using the equality comparer.

```
public static bool SequenceEqual<TSource>
(
   IEnumerable<TSource> first,
   IEnumerable<TSource> second
)
public static bool SequenceEqual<TSource>
(
   IEnumerable<TSource> first,
   IEnumerable<TSource> second,
   IEqualityComparer<TSource> comparer
)
```

Following is an example that compares two sequences using the `SequenceEqual` operator:

```
List<Icecreams> items1 = GetItems();
List<Icecreams> items2 = GetItems();
bool equal = items1.SequenceEqual(items2);
Console.WriteLine("The lists {0} equal.", equal ? "are" : "are not");
```

If the first or second element is null, `ArgumentNullExcpetion` is thrown.

Generation Operators

This operator is used for creating new sequences. The various generation operators are discussed in detail in the following sub-sections.

Empty

This operator returns an empty sequence of a given type.

```
public static IEnumerable<TResult> Empty<TResult> ()
```

If the object returned by this operator is enumerated, it yields nothing.

For example, the following code returns an empty sequence of type Item.

```
IEnumerable<Item> noItems = Enumerable.Empty<Item>();
Console.WriteLine(noItems.ToString());
```

Range

This operator is used to generate a sequence of integral numbers within a specified range.

```
public static IEnumerable<int> Range
(
    int start,
    int count
)
```

The code given below shows the use of Range operator to generate ten numbers.

```
IEnumerable<int> numbers = Enumerable.Range(1, 10);
foreach (int number in numbers)
Console.WriteLine(number);
```

ArgumentOutOfRangeException is thrown when the count is less than zero.

Repeat

This operator is used for generating a collection that contains repeated values.

```
public static IEnumerable<TResult> Repeat<TResult>
(
    TResult element,
    int count
)
```

The following code example demonstrates how to use the `Repeat` operator to generate a sequence of a repeated values. This code generates the same string, five times.

```
IEnumerable<string> strings = Enumerable.
  Repeat("Language Integrated Query", 5);
foreach (String str in strings)
  Console.WriteLine(str);
```

When the count is less than zero, `ArgumentOutOfRangeException` is thrown.

Quantifiers

This operator is used to find if any or all the elements in a sequence satisfy a specific condition.

All

The `All` operator is useful in determining whether all values in a collection satisfy a particular condition.

```
public static bool All<TSource>
(
  IEnumerable<TSource> source,
  Func<TSource, bool> predicate
)
```

This operator does not return any collection. It only returns true or false. The following code uses the `All` operator, which returns true if all the items category is equal to `Icecreams`.

```
List<Icecreams> items1 = GetItems();
bool all = items1.All(itm => itm.Category.Equals("Icecreams"));
Console.WriteLine("All Items are Icecreams ? {0}", all.ToString());
```

If the source element is null, `ArgumentNullException` is thrown.

Any

This is similar to the `All` operator, but it checks if any of the elements in a collection is equal to the specified value.

Following is the declaration of the `Any` operator to determine if the sequence contains any of the specified elements:

```
public static bool Any<TSource>
(
   IEnumerable<TSource> source
)
```

Following is the declaration of the `Any` operator to determine whether any of the elements in the sequence satisfy the condition.

```
public static bool Any<TSource>
(
IEnumerable<TSource> source,
Func<TSource, bool> predicate
)
```

The following example shows the use of `Any` operator to find if any of the items category is equal to `Pastrie`. If it is, it returns a true value.

```
List<Icecreams> items1 = GetItems();
bool any = items1.Any(itm => itm.Category.Equals("Pastries"));
Console.WriteLine("Item contains Pastries Also ? {0}",
   any.ToString());
```

`ArgumentNullException` is thrown if the source element is null.

Contains

This is similar to `Any` operator. It determines whether a sequence contains the specified element.

```
public static bool Contains<TSource>
(
   IEnumerable<TSource> source,
   TSource value
)
public static bool Contains<TSource>
(
   IEnumerable<TSource> source,
   TSource value,
   IEqualityComparer<TSource> comparer
)
```

The following example shows the code to check whether the specified item is present or not.

```
List<Icecreams> items = GetItems();
Icecreams itm = new Icecreams {Category="Icecreams", Name="Chocolate
    Fudge Icecream", Ingredients="cream, milk,
    mono and diglycerides...",
    Cholesterol="50mg", Protein="4g", TotalCarbohydrates="35g",
    TotalFat="20g", Price=10.5 };
    bool contains = items.Contains(itm);
```

If the value is null, `ArgumentNullException` is thrown.

Aggregation Operators

These operators are used to compute a value from a collection of values. For example, find the sum of all the numbers in a collection, or find the average of a collection of numbers. We will discuss all the aggregate operators in the following sub-sections:

Average

The `Average` operator is useful in computing an average value of a sequence of elements. This operator enumerates the source, invokes the selector function for each element, and computes the average of the resulting values.

If no selector function is specified, the average of the elements themselves is computed. An `ArgumentNullException` is thrown if any argument is null, and an `OverflowException` is thrown if the sum of the elements is too large.

Following is the code for calculating the average price of all ice-creams:

```
List<Item> items = GetItemsList();
var averageIcecreamsPrice = items.
Select(itm => new
{ itm.Name, averagePrice = itm.Price.Average(p => p.Price) });
```

Count

The Count operator is useful for counting the number of elements in a sequence.

```
public static int Count<TSource>
(
    IEnumerable<TSource> source
)
public static int Count<TSource>
(
    IEnumerable<TSource> source,
    Func<TSource, bool> predicate
)
```

If the source implements ICollection, the count can be obtained from the implementation itself.

ArgumentNullException is thrown if the source is null, and an OverflowException is thrown if the number of elements in the source is larger than the largest possible value of that type. This can be avoided by using LongCount.

LongCount

This is very similar to the Count method, but it can be used when we expect the result to be a large value.

Min

This operator finds the minimum value from a sequence of values. The Min operator enumerates the source sequence, invokes the selector function for each element and finds the minimum from a collection values.

```
public static decimal Min
(
    IEnumerable<T> source
)
public static S Min<TSource>
(
    IEnumerable<TSource> source,
    Func<TSource, S> selector
)
```

If a selector function is not specified, the minimum of the elements themselves is computed. If the values implement the IComparable<T> interface, the values are compared using it. Otherwise the values use the non-generic IComparable interface.

The following example uses the `Min` operator to find out the minimum value from a group of numbers.

```
int[] integers = { 5, 3, 8, 9, 1, 7};
int minNum = integers.Min();
Console.WriteLine("Minimum Number : {0}", minNum.ToString());
```

An `ArgumentNullException` is thrown if any of the arguments are null, and `InvalidOperationException` is thrown if the source contains no elements.

Max

This operator finds the maximum value from a sequence of values. The `Max` operator enumerates the source sequence, invokes the selector function for each element, and finds the maximum of the values.

```
public static decimal Max
(
    IEnumerable<T> source
)
public static S Max<TSource>
(
    Enumerable<TSource> source,
    Func<TSource, S> selector
)
```

If a selector function is not specified, the maximum of the elements themselves is computed. If the values implement the `IComparable<T>` interface, then the values are compared using it. If the values do not implement this interface then the non-generic `IComparable` interface is used for comparing the values.

The following example uses the `Max` operator to find out the maximum value from the group of numbers:

```
int[] integers = { 5, 3, 8, 9, 1, 7};
int maxNum = integers.Max();
Console.WriteLine("Maximum Number : {0}", maxNum.ToString());
```

If any of the arguments is null, then an `ArgumentNullException` is thrown, and `InvalidOperationException` is thrown if the source contains no elements.

Sum

This operator finds the total of the elements in a sequence. This Sum operator enumerates the source sequence, invokes the selector function for each element, and finds the total sum.

```
public static decimal Sum
(
    IEnumerable<T> source
)
public static S Sum<TSource> (
    IEnumerable<TSource> source,
    Func<TSource, S> selector
)
```

If a selector function is not specified, the sum of the elements themselves is computed.

The following example uses the Sum operator to find out the total of the given numbers:

```
int[] integers = { 5, 3, 8, 9, 1, 7};
int sum = integers.Sum();
Console.WriteLine("Total of all Numbers : {0}", sum.ToString());
```

If any of the arguments are null, an ArgumentNullException is thrown, and an OverflowException is thrown if the sum is larger than the maximum value for that type.

Aggregate

This operator applies a function over a sequence. It calls the function once for each element in the sequence. The first element of the source is the initial aggregate value. Every time the function is called, the operator passes the current element of the sequence to the function, and the current aggregated value as arguments. The first element of the source is the initial aggregated value. Every time the function returns a result, the previously aggregated value is replaced by the new value returned by it.

```
public static TSource Aggregate<TSource>
(
    IEnumerable<TSource> source,
    Func<TSource, TSource, TSource> func
)
public static TAccumulate Aggregate<TSource, TAccumulate>
(
    IEnumerable<TSource> source,
```

```
    TAccumulate seed,
    Func<TAccumulate, TSource, TAccumulate> func
)
public static TResult Aggregate<TSource, TAccumulate, TResult>
(
    IEnumerable<TSource> source,
    TAccumulate seed,
    Func<TAccumulate, TSource, TAccumulate> func,
    Func<TAccumulate, TResult> resultSelector
)
```

The following code is an example that shows how to change the order of strings.

```
string[] numbers = {"One", "Two", "Three", "Four", "Five",
    "Six", "Seven", "Eight", "Nine", "Ten"};
string reversedOrder = numbers.Aggregate((nums, next) =>
    next + " " + nums);
Console.WriteLine("Reversed using Aggregate: {0}", reversedOrder);
```

For every element in the sequence, the function which adds the values to the aggregate value is called. This happens for all the elements in the sequence. When we take the end result of the aggregate function, we will get the reversed order of the elements. The result would look like this:

```
Reversed using Aggregate: Ten Nine Eight Seven Six
Five Four Three Two One
```

If the source or function is null, `ArgumentNullException` is thrown, and an `InvalidOperationException` is thrown if the source does not contain any elements.

Partitioning Operators

These operators divide the input sequence into two or more sections, without rearranging the elements. Also, it returns only one of the sections and ignores the remaining elements.

Take

This operator returns only the specified number of elements from a sequence and skips the remaining elements. It starts from the beginning, and continues until the number is reached and then returns the elements.

It enumerates the source sequence and retrieves the elements one-by-one until the number of elements retrieved is equal to the number given by the count argument. If the count argument is less than or equal to zero, the sequence is not enumerated and no elements are returned.

```
public static IEnumerable<TSource> Take<TSource>
(
   IEnumerable<TSource> source,
   int count
)
```

The following code takes only five elements from a set of ten numbers.

```
int[] numbers = { 1, 2, 3, 4, 5, 6, 7, 8, 9, 10 };
var firstFive = numbers.Take(5);
foreach (int num in firstFive)
Console.WriteLine(num.ToString());
```

Following is another example for taking the first two ice-cream's objects from the list of objects retrieved using the `GetItems` method:

```
List<Icecreams> icecreams = GetItems();
IEnumerable<Icecreams> firstTwoIcecreams = icecreams.Take(2);
foreach (Icecreams ice in firstTwoIcecreams)
Console.WriteLine(ice.Name);
```

If the source is null, `ArgumentNullException` is thrown.

Skip

This operator is just the opposite of `Take` operator. It skips the specified number of elements in the sequence, and returns the remaining elements.

If the source sequence contains a lower number elements than the value specified by the count argument, it returns nothing. If the count argument is less than or equal to zero, it returns all the elements from the sequence.

```
public static IEnumerable<TSource> Skip<TSource>
(
   IEnumerable<TSource> source,
   int count
)
```

The following code skips the first five elements out of all the numbers, and returns the remaining numbers as sequence.

```
int[] numbers = { 1, 2, 3, 4, 5, 6, 7, 8, 9, 10};
var lastFive = numbers.Skip(5);
foreach (int num in lastFive)
Console.WriteLine(num.ToString());
```

An `ArgumentNullException` is thrown if the source is null.

TakeWhile

This operator returns elements from a sequence, while testing each element using the predicate function, and yields the element if the result is true. It fetches only those elements for which the function returns true.

```
public static IEnumerable<TSource> TakeWhile<TSource>
(
    IEnumerable<TSource> source,
    Func<TSource, bool> predicate
)
public static IEnumerable<TSource> TakeWhile<TSource>
(
    IEnumerable<TSource> source,
    Func<TSource, int, bool> predicate
)
```

The following code gets all the values that are less than five in the given sequence.

```
int[] numbers = { 1, 2, 3, 4, 5, 6, 7, 8, 9, 10 };
var firstFive = numbers.TakeWhile(num => num <= 5);
foreach (int num in firstFive)
Console.WriteLine(num.ToString());
```

This operator starts enumerating from the first element and continues until the function returns true. So in the above example, if the value is greater than five, it returns false and skips the elements after that.

SkipWhile

This operator starts enumerating a sequence, and skips all the elements while a specified condition is true, and then returns the remaining elements. The following code is a declaration where the first argument is the source sequence, and the second one is the predicate function to check against the source elements.

```
public static IEnumerable<TSource> SkipWhile<TSource>
(
    IEnumerable<TSource> source,
    Func<TSource, bool> predicate
)
```

Following is the declaration, similar to the above declaration but the integer used in the predicate function is the element index, in the sequence.

```
public static IEnumerable<TSource> SkipWhile<TSource>
(
    IEnumerable<TSource> source,
    Func<TSource, int, bool> predicate
)
```

The following code skips the first five elements and then retrieves the remaining elements in the sequences that are greater than five.

```
int[] numbers = { 1, 2, 3, 4, 5, 6, 7, 8, 9, 10 };
var lastFive = numbers.SkipWhile(num => num >5);
foreach (int num in lastFive)
Console.WriteLine(num.ToString());
```

`ArgumentNullException` is thrown if the source or the predicate function is null.

TakeWhile

This operator starts enumerating a sequence and takes all the elements while a specified condition is true, and then stops enumerating the remaining elements in the sequence. Given below is the syntax for `TakeWhile`, where the first argument is the source sequence and the second one is the predicate function to check against the source elements.

```
public static IEnumerable<TSource> TakeWhile<TSource>
(
    IEnumerable<TSource> source,
    Func<TSource, bool> predicate
)
```

Following is a declaration similar to the above declaration, but the integer used in the predicate function is the element index in the sequence.

```
public static IEnumerable<TSource> TakeWhile<TSource>
(
    IEnumerable<TSource> source,
    Func<TSource, int, bool> predicate
)
```

The following code takes all the items from a list, while the item with price more than 10 is reached. Here, you can see the descending order on the price of the items list to get all the items with price less than or equal to 10.

```
List<Item> items = GetItemsList();
List<Item> icecreamsWithLesserPrice = from itms in items
orderby itms.Price descending
select itms;
List<Item> topicecreamsWithLesserPrice = icecreamsWithLesserPrice.
TakeWhile(item => item.Price <= 10);
Console.WriteLine("Items with lesser price");
foreach (Item ItemswithLowPrice in icecreamsWithLesserPrice)
Console.WriteLine("Icecream Name: " + ItemswithLowPrice.Name + "
Price : " + ItemswithLowPrice.Price);
```

The variable, `topicecreamsWithLesserPrice` will contain only those items with price less than or equal to 10. Once the item with price greater than ten is found, all the remaining items will be ignored, including the first one which does not satisfy the condition.

Element Operators

These operators return a specific or a single element from a sequence.

DefaultIfEmpty

This operator is useful for replacing an empty sequence with a default value. When an object returned by `DefaultIfEmpty` is enumerated, it enumerates the source sequence object and retrieves its elements. If the source is empty, a single element with a default value is returned. The default value for reference and nullable types is null. An `ArgumentNullException` is thrown if the source is null.

```
public static IEnumerable<TSource> DefaultIfEmpty<TSource>
(
    IEnumerable<TSource> source
)
public static IEnumerable<TSource> DefaultIfEmpty<TSource>
(
    IEnumerable<TSource> source,
    TSource defaultValue
)
```

In the following example, we use the `defaultItem` argument. Then we define a list of items, which is an empty collection. After that, we try to enumerate through the object collection using `DefaultIfEmpty`. The `defaultItem` argument used for the operator, means that the default item defined is considered if the original sequence is empty.

```
Item defaultItem = new Item {Category="Icecreams", Name="Default
Item Test", Ingredients="cream, milk, ...", Cholesterol="50mg",
Protein="4g", TotalCarbohydrates="35g", TotalFat="20g", Price=10.5
, FatContents = new FatContent{SaturatedFat="6g", TransFat="4g",
OtherFat="6g"} };
List<Item> items = new List<Item>();
foreach (Item itm in items.DefaultIfEmpty(defaultItem))
Console.WriteLine("{0}", itm.Name);
```

An `ArgumentNullException` is thrown if the source argument is null.

ElementAt

This operator returns an element at a specified index in a sequence. It skips all the elements until the index is specified, and then returns the element from the specified index. If the source sequence implements `IList<T>`, the implementation is used for retrieving the element at the specified index.

```
public static TSource ElementAt<TSource>
(
   IEnumerable<TSource> source,
   int index
)
```

An `ArgumentNullException` is thrown if the source is null, and an `ArgumentOutOfRangeException` is thrown if the index value is less than zero or greater than or equal to the number of elements in source.

ElementAtOrDefault

This operator is a combination of `ElementAt` and `DefaultIFEmpty` operators. It checks for a specific item in the source. If it is empty, or the index is not found or out of range, it returns the default element.

```
public static TSource ElementAtOrDefault<TSource>
(
   IEnumerable<TSource> source,
   int index
)
```

The following code is gets the element at index fifteen, but we do not have that many names in the array specified, and because of that the operator `ElementAtOrDefault` will return a null to the string. We can check if the item is null or empty using the `IsNullOrEmpty` method and change the end result of the method.

```
string[] strings = { "Icecreams", "Pastries", "Buiscuits",
   "Chocolates", "Juices", "Fruits" };
int index = 15;
string name = strings.ElementAtOrDefault(index);
Console.WriteLine("The name at index {0} is '{1}'.",
index, String.IsNullOrEmpty(name) ? "<name not found at the specified
 index>" : name);
```

An `ArgumentNullException` is thrown if the source is null.

First

This `First` operator returns the very first element or the first element that satisfies a condition in a sequence.

```
public static TSource First<TSource>
(
   IEnumerable<TSource> source
)
public static TSource First<TSource>
(
   IEnumerable<TSource> source,
   Func<TSource, bool> predicate
)
```

Following is an example which shows how to retrieve the first element from a list, with and without using a condition.

```
int[] numbers = { 1, 2, 3, 4, 5, 6, 7, 8, 9, 10 };
int firstNumber = numbers.First();
Console.WriteLine("The First number in the list is: {0}", firstNumber.
ToString());
int firstNumberwithCondition = numbers.First(num => num == 10);
Console.WriteLine("The First number in the list which satifies the
condition is: {0}", firstNumberwithCondition.ToString());
```

An `ArgumentNullException` is thrown if the source is null.

FirstOrDefault

This operator is very similar to the `First` operator, but it returns the default value if the source does not have any elements in it.

```
public static TSource FirstOrDefault<TSource>
(
    IEnumerable<TSource> source
)
public static TSource FirstOrDefault<TSource>
(
    IEnumerable<TSource> source,
    Func<TSource, bool> predicate
)
```

In the following code, `FirstOrDefault` returns a default value if the source sequence does not have any value. In the first example, the integer array is empty. The `FirstOrDefault` operator returns a zero in this case.

```
int[] numbers = {};
int firstNumber = numbers.FirstOrDefault();
Console.WriteLine("The First number in the list is: {0}",
    firstNumber);
```

The following example shows an empty string array. In this case, the operator returns nothing. We can check the value using `IsNullOrEmpty`, and then return the default value or a message.

```
string[] strings = { };
string firstStringwithCondition = strings.FirstOrDefault(str =>
str == "Chocolate");
Console.WriteLine("{0}",
    string.IsNullOrEmpty(firstStringwithCondition) ? "Source is Empty" :
    firstStringwithCondition);
```

An `ArgumentNullException` is thrown if the source is null.

Last

This operator returns the last element, or the last element which satisfies a predicate condition.

```
public static TSource Last<TSource>
(
    IEnumerable<TSource> source
)
```

```
public static TSource Last<TSource>
(
    IEnumerable<TSource> source,
    Func<TSource, bool> predicate
)
```

The following code shows how to get the last element from a sequence, and also the last element in the sequence that satisfies the given condition.

```
int[] numbers = { 1, 2, 3, 4, 5, 6, 7, 8, 9, 10, 11,
    12, 13, 14, 15 };
int lastNumber = numbers.Last();
Console.WriteLine("The last number in the list is: {0}", lastNumber.
ToString());
int lastNumberwithCondition = numbers.Last(num => num == 10);
Console.WriteLine("The last number in the list
which satisfies the condition is: {0}",
    lastNumberwithCondition.ToString());
```

An `ArgumentNullException` is thrown if the source is null, and the `InvalidOperationException` is thrown if none of the elements satisfy the condition, or the source sequence is empty.

LastOrDefault

This operator is very similar to the `Last` operator, but it returns a default if the source does not have any element in it.

```
public static TSource LastOrDefault<TSource>
(
    IEnumerable<TSource> source
)
public static TSource LastOrDefault<TSource>
(
    IEnumerable<TSource> source,
    Func<TSource, bool> predicate
)
```

In the following code, `LastOrDefault` returns the default value if the source sequence does not have any value. In the first example, the integer array is empty. The `LastOrDefault` operator returns zero in this case.

```
int[] numbers = {};
int lastNumber = numbers.LastOrDefault();
Console.WriteLine("The Last number in the list is: {0}", lastNumber);
```

The next shows the empty string array. In this case, the operator returns nothing. We can check the value using the `IsNullOrEmpty` operator and then return the default value or message required.

```
string[] strings = { };
string lastStringwithCondition = strings.LastOrDefault(str => str ==
  "Chocolate");
Console.WriteLine("{0}",

  string.IsNullOrEmpty(lastStringwithCondition) ? "Source is Empty" :

  lastStringwithCondition);
```

An `ArgumentNullException` is thrown if the source is null.

Single

This operator returns a single element from a sequence. If there is more then one element in the sequence, we should use a condition to get a single element from the list.

```
public static TSource Single<TSource>
(
    IEnumerable<TSource> source
)
public static TSource Single<TSource>
(
    IEnumerable<TSource> source,
    Func<TSource, bool> predicate
)
```

The following code gets a single element, using a condition from the sequence.

```
int[] numbers = { 12};
int singleNumber = numbers.Single();
Console.WriteLine("The Single number is: {0}",
  singleNumber.ToString());
int singleNumberwithCondition = numbers.Single(num => num == 12);
Console.WriteLine("Single number in the list which satifies the
condition is: {0}", singleNumberwithCondition.ToString());
```

In the above example, if the sequence is like `int[] numbers = {12, 13, 14 , 15, 12}`, then the `Single` operator throws an exception.

An `ArgumentNullException` is thrown if the source is null and an `InvalidOperationException` is thrown if no element satisfies the condition, more than one element satisfies the condition, or the source is empty.

SingleOrDefault

This operator is similar to the `Single` operator that returns a single element in the sequence, but the difference is the `SingleOrDefault` will return the default value if the source does not have any element in it.

```
public static TSource SingleOrDefault<TSource>
(
    IEnumerable<TSource> source
)
public static TSource SingleOrDefault<TSource>
(
    IEnumerable<TSource> source,
    Func<TSource, bool> predicate
)
```

The following example uses the `SingleOrDefault` operator to fetch a single element from the sequence. It returns the default value, zero, if the integer array is empty.

```
int[] numbers = { };
int singleNumber = numbers.SingleOrDefault();
Console.WriteLine("The Single number in the list is: {0}",

    singleNumber);
```

The following code has a condition to fetch the element from the sequence. It returns null if the sequence does not have any element in it. So we can use the `IsNullOrEmpty` operator to check the null value, and then return a custom message or value.

```
string[] strings = { };
string singleStringwithCondition = strings.SingleOrDefault(str =>
str == "Chocolate");
            Console.WriteLine("{0}", string.IsNullOrEmpty(singleSt
ringwithCondition) ? "Source is Empty":
  singleStringwithCondition);
```

An `ArgumentNullException` is thrown if the source is null, and `InvalidOperationException` is thrown if more than one element satisfies the condition.

List of Query Operators

Operator Type	Operator	Description
Restriction	Where	Filters elements.
	OfType	Filters elements based on their type in the collection.
Projection	Select	Selects values.
	SelectMany	Selects values and combines the resulting collections into one collection.
Join	Join	Joins two sequences based on matching keys and extracts a pair of values from different sources of data.
	GroupJoin	Joins two sequences based on matching keys and groups the resulting matches.
Concatenation	Concat	Concatenates two different collections of data into one.
Ordering	OrderBy	Sorts the resulting values in ascending order.
	OrderByDescending	Sorts resulting values in descending order.
	ThenBy	Performs a secondary sort in ascending order.
	ThenByDescending	Performs secondary sort in descending order.
	Reverse	Reverses the order of the elements in a collection.
Set	Distinct	Removes duplicate values, and returns unique values from a collection.
	Except	Returns only those elements from a collection that do not appear in another collection.
	Intersect	Returns only those elements that are common to both collections
	Union	Returns those elements that appear in either of the two collections. This is a combination of both the collections containing unique elements.
Grouping	GroupBy	Returns grouped elements that are having a common key.

Operator Type	Operator	Description
Conversion	AsEnumerable	Returns the input typed as `IEnumerable<T>`.
	Cast	Casts the element to a specified type.
	OfType	This is to filter the values depending on the ability of the values to be cast to a specified type.
	ToArray	Converts a collection into an array.
	ToDictionary	Puts elements into a dictionary.
	ToList	Converts a collection into a list.
	ToLookup	Puts elements into a lookup, which is a one-to-many dictionary.
Equality	SequenceEqual	Determines whether two collections are equal by comparing the elements.
Element	DefaultIfEmpty	If the collection is empty, it will be replaced with a default valued single collection.
	ElementAt	Returns the element at a specified index in the collection.
	ElementAtOrDefault	Returns an element from a specified index or a default value, if the index is out of range.
	First	Returns the first element in a collection or the first element that satisfies a condition.
	FirstOrDefault	Returns the first element or the first element in a collection that satisfies a condition. If the first element is empty, it returns the default value. This is the combination of `First` and DefaultIfEmpty operators.
	Last	Returns the last element or the last element that satisfies the condition in a collection.
	LastOrDefault	Returns the last element or the last element that satisfies a condition. If the last element is empty, it returns the default value.
	Single	Returns the only element or the only element in a collection which satisfies the condition.
	SingleOrDefault	Returns the only element or the only element in a collection that satisfies the condition. If no such elements exists or if the collection does not contain exactly one element, return the default value.

Operator Type	Operator	Description
Generation	Empty	Returns an empty collection.
	Range	Generates a collection that contains a sequence of numbers.
	Repeat	Generates a collection that contains one repeated value.
Quantifiers	All	Determines whether all values in a collection satisfy the condition.
	Any	Determines whether any of the values in a collection satisfy the condition.
	Contains	Determines whether the collection contains any element which is specified.
Aggregation	Aggregate	Accumulates all the values in a collection.
	Average	Calculates the average of all the values in a collection.
	Count	Counts the number of elements that satisfy a condition in a collection.
	LongCount	Counts the number of elements that satisfy a condition in a large collection.
	Max	Determines the maximum value in a collection.
	Min	Determines a minimum value in a collection.
	Sum	Calculates the sum of all the values in a collection.
Partitioning	Skip	Skips elements in a collection up to the specified number
	SkipWhile	Skips elements in a collection while an element in the collection does not satisfy a condition.
	Take	Takes all the elements up to a specified position in the collection
	Takewhile	Takes elements in a collection, while an element in the collection does not satisfy the condition.

Query Operator Equivalent Expressions

Some of the important query operators have equivalent query expressions. A query expression is a more readable form of query. At compile time, these expressions are translated into calls to the corresponding query methods. The following table shows the list of equivalent expressions for some of the query operators.

Query Operator	Equivalent Expression
Cast	Use explicitly typed range variable
GroupBy	Group by (or) Group by…into This is for grouping of objects
GroupJoin	Join…in…on…equals…into
Join	Join…in…on…equals
OrderBy	Order by
OrderByDescending	Order by…descending
Select	select
SelectMany	Multiple from clauses
Where	where
ThenBy	Order by
ThenByDescending	Order by…, …descending

Summary

In this chapter, we have seen different query operators supported by LINQ. These operators can be used on the objects whose type implements the `IEnumerable<T>` interface, or the interface `IQueryable<T>`. All operators differ from one another with respect to the time of execution. The operators like `Average` and `Sum`, which return a single value, will execute immediately, whereas operators like `Select`, `SelectMany`, `TakeWhile`, will defer the query execution and return an enumerable object. We can also replace standard query operators with our own implementation that provides additional required services.

Building an ASP.NET Application

In this book we have seen how to use LINQ to Objects, SQL, Dataset, XML and XSD. We have also seen a number of examples for different query operators used by LINQ. Now, in this appendix, we will see how we can use LINQ features to make web application development easier. Let's build a simple ASP.NET application with one page having a drop-down, and a grid to show details corresponding to the selection of the drop-down box.

On selecting a particular category, we should be able to get the list of items for the selected category in the grid. Let us see how we can build this web application in Visual Studio using LINQ.

Create a new ASP.NET web application using **File | New | Web Site | ASP.NET Web Site**, as shown in the following screenshot:

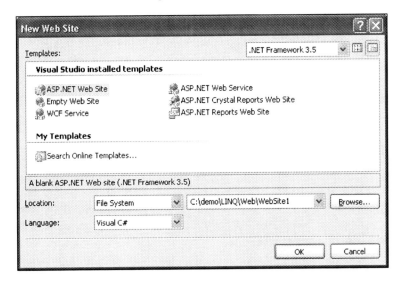

Following are the default references that get added to a project when we create it. To make use of LINQ to SQL, we need to add some additional references to the project, specifically **System.Data.Linq** and **System.Data**.

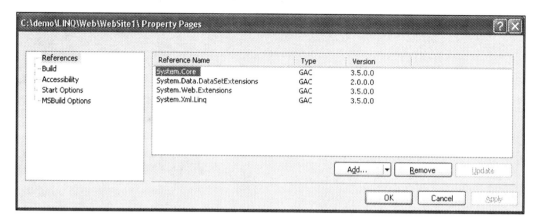

Also add the following namespaces to the project. This will let you use LINQ for querying data from the database.

```
using System.Data.Linq;
using System.Data.Linq.Mapping;
```

Now we have to create the required database entity objects for our web application. Create the database objects with properties as shown below:

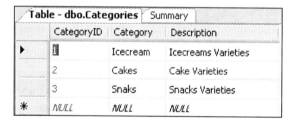

The above database objects can be created using LINQ to SQL queries. For more information on this, please see Chapter 4, *LINQ to SQL*. Let's consider that we have these database objects ready. Now we have to create classes that map to the above database objects and the database.

```csharp
[Database(Name = "Deserts")]
public class Deserts : DataContext
{
  public Table<Categories> Categories;
  public Table<Items> Items;
  public Deserts(string connection) : base(connection) { }
}
[Table(Name = "Categories")]
public class Categories
{
  [Column(Name = "CategoryID", IsPrimaryKey = true,
    IsDbGenerated = true, DbType = "int NOT NULL IDENTITY",
    CanBeNull = false)]
  public int CategoryID
  {
    get;
    private set;
  }
  [Column(Name = "Category", DbType = "nvarchar(1000)")]
  public string Category
  {
    get;
    set;
  }
  [Column(Name = "Description", DbType = "nvarchar(1000)",
    UpdateCheck = UpdateCheck.Never)]
  public string Description
  {
    get;
    set;
  }
  private EntitySet<Items> _Items;
  [Association(Name = "FK_Category_Items", Storage = "_Items",
    OtherKey = "CategoryID", IsForeignKey = true)]
  public EntitySet<Items> Items
  {
    get { return this._Items; }
    set { this._Items.Assign(value); }
  }
  public Categories() { this._Items = new EntitySet<Items>(); }
}
[Table(Name = "Items")]
public class Items
{
```

```
    [Column(Name = "ItemID", IsPrimaryKey = true, IsDbGenerated = true,
      DbType = "int NOT NULL IDENTITY", CanBeNull = false)]
    public int ItemID { get; private set; }
    [Column(Name = "CategoryID")]
    public int CategoryID { get; set; }
    [Column(Name = "Name", DbType = "nvarchar(1000)")]
     public string Name { get; set; }
    [Column(Name = "Ingredients", DbType = "nvarchar(1000)")]
    public string Ingredients { get; set; }
    [Column(Name = "ServingSize", DbType = "nvarchar(1000)")]
    public string ServingSize { get; set; }
    [Column(Name = "TotalFat", DbType = "nvarchar(1000)")]
    public string TotalFat { get; set; }
    [Column(Name = "Cholesterol", DbType = "nvarchar(1000)")]
    public string Cholesterol { get; set; }
    [Column(Name = "TotalCarbohydrates", DbType = "nvarchar(1000)")]
    public string TotalCarbohydrates { get; set; }
    [Column(Name = "Protein", DbType = "nvarchar(1000)")]
    public string Protein { get; set; }
    private EntityRef<Categories> _Categories;
    [Association(Name = "FK_Category_Items", Storage = "_Categories",
    ThisKey = "CategoryID", IsForeignKey = true)]
      public Categories Categories
      {
          get { return this._Categories.Entity; }
          set { this._Categories.Entity = value; }
      }
    public Items() { this._Categories = new EntityRef<Categories>(); }
}
```

The above code creates mapping of:

1. `Deserts` class to the `Deserts` SQL database. This class is of type `DataContext`.

2. `Categories` class to the `Categories` SQL database object in the `Deserts` database.

3. `Items` class to the `Items` SQL database object in the `Deserts` database.

We also need to have primary and foreign keys defined for these classes.

Now open the `Default.aspx` designer and add the following controls to build the web page:

1. Add the HTML table to design the UI.

2. Add a **Label** and a **DropDownList** to the page for categories selection.

3. Add a button control to execute LINQ queries, and bind the results to the **GridView** control.

4. Add a **GridView** control to show **List of Items** for the selected category in the drop down list.

5. Add a **Label** and a **TextBox** control to show **Total Items** for the selected category.

After adding all the controls to the web page, it would look like this:

Category	Unbound	▼	Get Items

List of Items

Name	Category	Protein	Ingredients
Databound	Databound	Databound	Databound
Databound	Databound	Databound	Databound
Databound	Databound	Databound	Databound
Databound	Databound	Databound	Databound
Databound	Databound	Databound	Databound

Total Items : 0

The columns shown in GridView correspond to the details that will be fetched for the selected category using LINQ queries. We can also set GridView's properties to automatically generate columns at runtime.

```
<asp:GridView ID="GridView1" runat="server" Width="936px" AutoGenerateColumns="False"
              BorderColor="Black" BorderStyle="Solid" BorderWidth="2px" CellPadding="1"
              ForeColor="Black">
<Columns>
   <asp:BoundField HeaderText="Name" DataField="Name" HeaderStyle-Width="20%" />
   <asp:BoundField HeaderText="Category" DataField="Category" HeaderStyle-Width="10%" />
   <asp:BoundField HeaderText="Protein" DataField="Protein" HeaderStyle-Width="10%" />
   <asp:BoundField HeaderText="Ingredients" DataField="Ingredients" HeaderStyle-Width="60%" />
</Columns>

</asp:GridView>
```

Add the following code to the constructor of the class to create a connection to the Deserts database, and this will also create an object using the Deserts DataContext. The Deserts variable can be declared as public, as it is referred to throughout the application.

```
public Deserts dataBase;
Deserts database = new Deserts("Data Source=.\sqlexpress;Initia
   Catalog=Deserts;Integrated Security=true");
```

Now add the following code to the `Page_Init` event of the page to load the categories drop-down. We will also make use of a LINQ to SQL query to fetch the list of categories from the database.

```
protected void Page_Init(object sender, EventArgs e)
{
    var icecreams = from cat in dataBase.Categories
    select cat.Category;
    DropDownList1.DataSource = icecreams;
    DropDownList1.DataBind();
    lblCount.Visible = false;
    lblTotalItems.Visible = false;
}
```

Now save the application and execute it. We can see the web page with the drop-down list loaded with a list of categories as shown in the following figure:

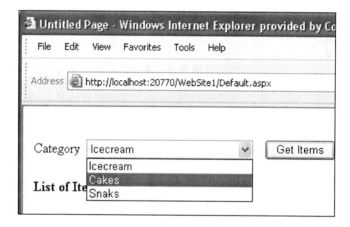

You will also need to write code for getting items for the selected category that form the drop-down list. Add the following code to the **Get Items** button control:

```
protected void Button1_Click(object sender, EventArgs e)
{
    GridView1.DataSource = from items in dataBase.Items
    join categories in dataBase.Categories on items.CategoryID
        equals categories.CategoryID
    where categories.Category == DropDownList1.SelectedValue.ToString()
    select new { items.Name, items.Categories.Category,
        items.Protein, items.Ingredients };
    GridView1.DataBind();
```

```
int iCount = (from items in dataBase.Items
join categories in dataBase.Categories on items.CategoryID
  equals categories.CategoryID
where categories.Category == DropDownList1.SelectedValue.ToString()
select new { items.Name, items.Categories.Category,
items.Protein, items.Ingredients }).Count();
if (iCount > 0)
{
  lblCount.Visible = true;
  lblTotalItems.Visible = true;
  lblCount.Text = iCount.ToString();
}
else
{
  lblCount.Visible = false;
  lblTotalItems.Visible = false;
}
}
```

In the above code, the source for `GridView1` is a LINQ query which fetches all items for the selected category. The same query with the `Count` operator is used for getting the total number items retrieved for the selected category.

The final output of the web page would be as follows:

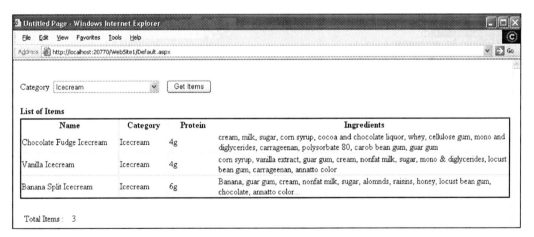

B

LINQ with Outlook

In this appendix we will make use of LINQ to access an Outlook object and get details of contacts.

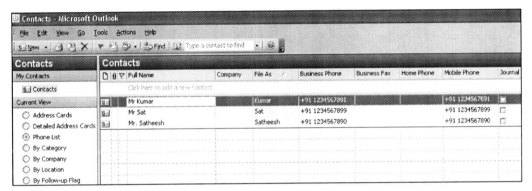

Create a new .NET Console application using the **File | New | Project | Windows | Console application** option in Visual Studio. Add a reference to the Outlook Object Library to the project folder, as shown below.

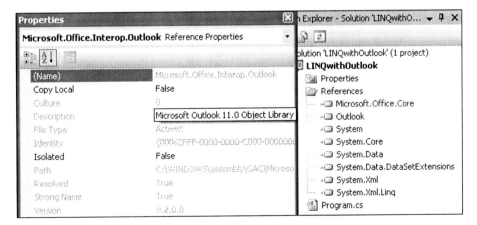

The above image shows **Microsoft Outlook 11.0 Object Library** added to the project. This provides an interface to access Outlook properties, which will let us collect contact information from Outlook.

Add the following namespace to the project:

```
using Microsoft.Office.Interop.Outlook;
```

Now add the following code to the `Main` method of the project:

```
_Application outlook = new Application();
// Contacts
MAPIFolder folder = outlook.ActiveExplorer().Session
   .GetDefaultFolder(OlDefaultFolders.olFolderContacts);
var contacts = from contact in folder.Items.OfType<ContactItem>()
select contact;
foreach (var contact in contacts)
{
   Console.WriteLine(contact.FirstName);
}
```

The above code references the **Contacts** folder. A LINQ query is used to access contact details from the folder by enumerating through the `Items` of type `ContactItem`.

Each item within the **Contacts** list has different properties that can be seen when we create a new contact in Outlook.

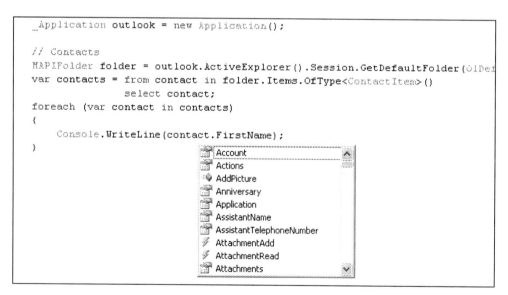

In the example we are collecting the **FirstName** of all the contacts in the contacts list. The output of the example would be:

```
ca   file:///c:/demo/LINQ/Web/LINQwithOutlook/LINQwithOutlook/bin/D
Satheesh
Sat
Kumar
```

LINQ queries can also be used to access addresses, tasks, mails, etc. The following code shows a query for collecting details from the address book.

```
// Addresses
var addresses = from address in folder.Items.OfType<AddressList>()
select address;
foreach (var addres in addresses)
{
   Console.WriteLine(addres.Name);
}
```

LINQ queries are not only used for accessing XML, database and Outlook objects, but also to access information from Microsoft Excel, Microsoft Project, Microsoft Word and others.

Index

About Packt Publishing

Packt, pronounced 'packed', published its first book "*Mastering phpMyAdmin for Effective MySQL Management*" in April 2004 and subsequently continued to specialize in publishing highly focused books on specific technologies and solutions.

Our books and publications share the experiences of your fellow IT professionals in adapting and customizing today's systems, applications, and frameworks. Our solution based books give you the knowledge and power to customize the software and technologies you're using to get the job done. Packt books are more specific and less general than the IT books you have seen in the past. Our unique business model allows us to bring you more focused information, giving you more of what you need to know, and less of what you don't.

Packt is a modern, yet unique publishing company, which focuses on producing quality, cutting-edge books for communities of developers, administrators, and newbies alike. For more information, please visit our website: www.packtpub.com.

Writing for Packt

We welcome all inquiries from people who are interested in authoring. Book proposals should be sent to authors@packtpub.com. If your book idea is still at an early stage and you would like to discuss it first before writing a formal book proposal, contact us; one of our commissioning editors will get in touch with you.

We're not just looking for published authors; if you have strong technical skills but no writing experience, our experienced editors can help you develop a writing career, or simply get some additional reward for your expertise.

PUBLISHING

ODP.NET Developer's Guide

ISBN: 978-1-847191-96-0   Paperback: 300 pages

A practical guide for developers working with the Oracle Data Provider for .NET and the Oracle Developer Tools for Visual Studio 2005

1. Application development with ODP.NET

2. Dealing with XML DB using ODP.NET

3. Oracle Developer Tools for Visual Studio .NET

Learning jQuery

ISBN: 978-1-847192-50-9   Paperback: 380 pages

jQuery: Better Interaction Design and Web Development with Simple JavaScript Techniques

1. Create better, cross-platform JavaScript code

2. Detailed solutions to specific client-side problems

Please check **www.PacktPub.com** for information on our titles

Programming Windows Workflow Foundation

ISBN: 978-1-904811-21-3   Paperback: 300 pages

A C# developer's guide to the features and programming interfaces of Windows Workflow Foundation

1. Add event-driven workflow capabilities to your .NET applications.

2. Highlights the libraries, services and internals programmers need to know

3. Builds a practical "bug reporting" workflow solution example app

Programming Microsoft® Dynamics™ NAV

ISBN: 978-1-904811-74-9   Paperback: 480 pages

Create, modify, and maintain applications in NAV 5.0, the latest version of the ERP application formerly known as Navision

1. For experienced programmers with little or no previous knowledge of NAV development

2. Learn as quickly as possible to create, modify, and maintain NAV applications

3. Written for version 5.0 of NAV; applicable for all versions

Please check **www.PacktPub.com** for information on our titles

LaVergne, TN USA
24 October 2010

201945LV00005B/35/A